PROFESSIONAL ENGLISH

Communication skills for professionals
working in business, industry and
international organisations

Coursebook

Mark Ellis, Nina O'Driscoll and Adrian Pilbeam
Language Training Services

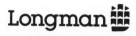
Longman

Longman Group UK Limited
Longman House, Burnt Mill, Harlow,
Essex CM20 2JE, England
and Associated Companies throughout the world.

First published 1984
Seventh impression 1992

ISBN 0-582-74882-8

Set in 9/11pt Linotron 202 Rockwell Light
Produced by Longman Group (FE) Ltd
Printed in Hong Kong

Acknowledgements
We are grateful to the following for permission to reproduce copyright illustrative material:

Advertising Standards Authority for page 57; Art Directors Photo Library for page 85;
Aspect Picture Library Limited for page 40 (bottom); British Petroleum plc for page 87;
Britoil plc for page 63 (right); British Steel Corporation for page 21; Casio Electronics
Company Limited for the modified advertisement on page 68; Colour Library International
Limited for page 40 (top); Daily Telegraph Colour Library for page 79; Ian Dobbie/
Personal Computer World for page 98; 'Based on charts published in the Economist
Newspapers' for pages 52 (top) and 62 (top right and bottom); Esso Petroleum Company
Limited for page 63 (left); Financial Times for page 52 (middle and bottom) and Financial
Times/Book Marketing Council for page 62 (top left); Ford Motor Company Limited for
page 86; Longman Photo Unit for pages 1, 12, 14, 23, 33, 35, 73, 80 and 117; Media
Expenditure Analysis for page 60; The Photographers Library for page 31.

Our special thanks to the American Express Company, Barclays Bank plc, British Airways,
Diners Club International, McGraw Hill Inc, National Westminster Bank plc, W.H. Smith
and Son Limited and Trans World Airlines Inc.

Cover photograph by The Image Bank of Photography (Photo Bill Carter)

We have been unable to trace the copyright holder of the two charts on page 88, and
would be grateful for any information that would enable us to do so.

Artists Michael ffolkes, John Fraser and Oxford Illustrators

CONTENTS

iii

INTRODUCTION

What is it and who is it for?

Professional English is a flexible business and professional English Language course. It is designed for people working in business, industry and related professional fields, and can also be used by students of business. The material can be used at both intermediate and advanced level.

Objectives

The main aims of the course are:

— to revise and consolidate important language structures and functions

— to develop skills in dealing with more complex language

— to increase awareness of the appropriate language to use in a range of social, professional, formal and informal situations

— to improve communication skills in meetings, discussions, presentations, telephoning, social contacts and the writing of short memos, telexes, letters and reports

Content

There are ten units covering broad themes relevant to most job functions and industry sectors including Innovation, Image, Quality Control, Information Flow and Future Developments. In addition there are three case-studies. Each unit has four parts:

— Language Review, for consolidation of 'old' language

— Language Study, for acquisition of 'new' language

— Focus on Interaction, for development of communication skills

— Activities, for open-ended practice

Language activities include problem-solving, information transfer tasks, role plays and transfer to students' own work environment. Most of the material has been drawn from real business cases, and to reflect the realities of multi-national communication and discussions, presentations and phone conversations on tape include English, American and non-native speakers of English.

Use of the material

Professional English is designed for use with a teacher, either in small groups or individually. The material has been designed with flexibility in mind – each unit and often each part of each unit are free-standing, and can be used in any order and combination. The course can therefore be used:

— on one or two day intensive sessions devoted to single communication skills such as meetings, presentations or telephoning

— on five or ten day intensive courses held in-company

— on longer extensive courses

Full information on 'routes through the book' can be found in the accompanying Teaching Guide.

1   A QUESTION OF COMPANY STRUCTURE

LANGUAGE REVIEW: Asking questions; Describing change; Comparing information

Asking questions

1   With a colleague, you are reviewing the salaries and job definitions of several people in the company. For one of these people, John Robinson, your colleague has all the relevant information. (In the Teaching Guide.) Ask questions to find out:

a   his responsibilities, present salary, boss, date of joining the company, length of time in this job, amount of holidays, sickness record

b   if he has had a salary increase in the last 12 months
if he has a company car
if he travels abroad on business
if his present boss recommends promotion
if he is hardworking and reliable

2   Now obtain personal and job related information about other people.

Your questions should cover the following subjects:

place of work – which company
job
particular responsibilities
difficult aspects of the job
length of time in this job or company
previous experience
family – married, single, children
location of home
interests and hobbies
particular likes and dislikes

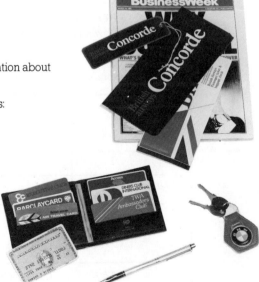

3 Below you will find information about Taga, a Japanese electronics company. The information is in the column on the left. Choose questions from the right hand column which will produce this information.

Information	Questions
11,392	Where are your headquarters?
TV's and domestic appliances	What was your turnover last year?
60 miles outside Tokyo	How many departments are there?
1951	Who are your main competitors?
No, not at the moment	What do you produce?
$206.4 m	When did you introduce robots?
Sony and Hitachi	Where do you export to?
five	When was the company set up?
1978	Do you want to open a factory in Great Britain?
Mostly to Europe	How many people do you employ?

4 Imagine you need to find information from the public about a consumer product or service, e.g. video recorders, toothpaste, a magazine, auto-banks. Build up a questionnaire to get this information. Consider the following factors, among others:

price, frequency of use, type of use, content, style, size, packaging

Describing change

Regine Klaus, Heidi Heinig and Johannes Schmidt are members of a German research team working in the laboratory of S.P.O.T., a company which produces cosmetics. The diagram below gives you some information about their present and past jobs.

1 Ask questions to complete the information.

		responsible for buying new testing equipment	supervisor of all lab tests and trials	Regine
at school				Heidi
	with Bloom, another cosmetic co.			Johannes
5 years ago	1 year ago	6 months ago	now	

2   Read the extracts from the two personal profiles below.
Use this information to complete the notes in the right hand
column.

Extract 1	Event	Time
Before he joined Delta Motors last year, Bob Masters worked for several years at the Foley plant of Universal Motors. There he was responsible for designing many of the features of the Bandit as well as other major Universal Motor models. Bob Masters is a most welcome addition to our design team at Delta Motors. He is now working on the Supreme but we all hope he has time to continue his golfing activities. Bob is married and his wife Mary had a baby boy last winter.	joined DM worked for UM	last year before
		now
		last winter
Extract 2		
Tom Keith succeeds David Brown as Manager of the European Division at the Banks HQ in London. Tom began his banking career in 1948 in the Croydon Branch, and three years later he was appointed Asst. Manager. During the next 15 years he held a number of management posts including that of Section Manager in the Overseas Department. In the autumn of 1963 he was transferred to our branch in Zurich and the following year he spent in Brussels. In 1965 he returned to the UK where he worked in the European section until he was promoted a month ago.		in 1948 3 years later during the next 15 years
		in the autumn of 1963
		the following year in 1965
		a month ago

3   Look at the chart below which gives some information
about the development of Delta Motors. Ask questions about
these developments in order to complete the chart. The
information is in the Teaching Guide.

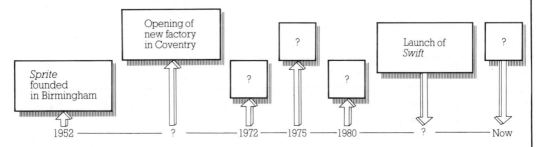

Notes

1952 –19 ? : Period of expansion for *Sprite*

1960 –19 ? : Period of high sales and good profits
for *Sprite*

19 ? – now: Recession in Europe generally and in
the car industry. Decline in activities
of Delta Motors

Comparing information

1 *You will hear an extract from the Chairman's address at the AGM of Garfield Inc. He is comparing the performance of two subsidiaries, one in Bogota, Colombia and the other in Turin, Italy.*

1   Complete the chart below and then decide which of the subsidiaries has the better performance in each of the categories.

	Bogota	Turin
Production		
Strikes		
Financial results		
Market share		
Labour costs		

2   Match the caption with the cartoon.

There are fewer people working than before.

There isn't half as much paperwork with a computer as with manual systems.

Decision-making is considerably quicker than it was before.

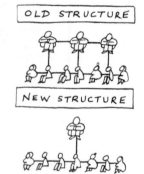

3   You are preparing a report on three large companies in the packaged food and grocery products sector. Present a summary of your findings from the information in the chart below.

	Company A	Company B	Company C
Number of employees worldwide 1982	47,000	52,000	11,000
Number of employees worldwide 1983	+10%	+6%	+8%
Turnover 1982	$3,500m	$3,400m	$2,500m
Profit 1982	$160.4m	$65.4m	$89.2m
Profit 1983	+5%	+6%	+10%
% female workers	55%	60%	45%

4   Look at the charts below which are taken from the
Annual Report of a Swedish Pharmaceutical Company. What
are the interesting points of comparison?

Employees based in Sweden — level of education

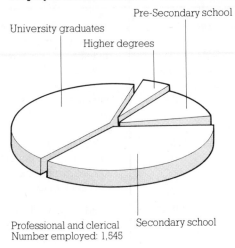

Professional and clerical
Number employed: 1,545

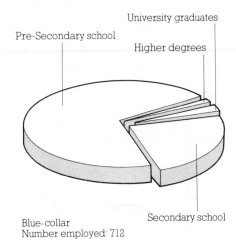

Blue-collar
Number employed: 712

LANGUAGE STUDY: Showing contrast and similarity

Showing contrast and similarity

*Frieda Mühren, who works for a Dutch chemical company,
has recently been promoted.*

2   **1**   Listen to her talking about the changes in her job, and
complete the following chart.

	1977	*Now*
Job title	Marketing Assistant	
Department		Marketing
Duties		
Special responsibilities		
Responsible for	Member of a team	
Responsible to		

The notes below show some of the similarities and differences in her work. Look particularly at the words which show whether something is the same or different. These words are in **bold type.**

Before	Now	
Analysed and collected data	Supervises product ranges	Her present duties are very **different from** her previous duties.
Gaining experience	In charge of soap and hair care products	Now she is in charge of both the soap range and hair care products, **whereas** before she was gaining experience.
Worked as a team member	Leads a team of five	Before she worked as a member of a team, **but** now she has five people working for her.
Low level of responsibility	High level of responsibility. Work very varied	In her new job she has greater responsibility than before. **On the other hand** the work is more varied.
40 hours a week at work	40 hours a week at work	The hours she spends at work are **the same as** before.
Finishes work at 6	Finishes work at 6. Takes work home.	She finishes work at the same time as before. **However**, now she also takes work home.

2   The diagram below shows changes in the structure of a company. Describe the differences and similarities between the present situation and the situation as it was. Use appropriate words and phrases to show contrast and similarity.

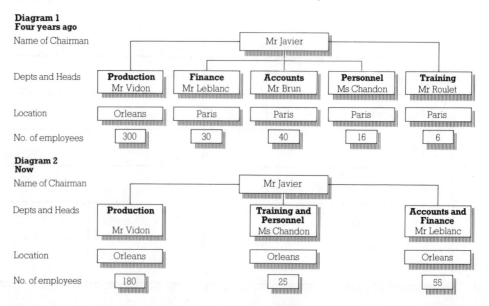

Diagram 1
Four years ago

Name of Chairman			Mr Javier		
Depts and Heads	**Production** Mr Vidon	**Finance** Mr Leblanc	**Accounts** Mr Brun	**Personnel** Ms Chandon	**Training** Mr Roulet
Location	Orleans	Paris	Paris	Paris	Paris
No. of employees	300	30	40	16	6

Diagram 2
Now

Name of Chairman		Mr Javier	
Depts and Heads	**Production** Mr Vidon	**Training and Personnel** Ms Chandon	**Accounts and Finance** Mr Leblanc
Location	Orleans	Orleans	Orleans
No. of employees	180	25	55

3   The notes below compare the working week and paid holidays in various parts of the world. These notes are written out in full in Text 1 using linking words to emphasise points of similarity and difference. Pick out these linking words.

Working Week		Annual Paid Holiday	
Most of Europe/N. America	40 hours	North America	10–20 days
Switzerland	43 hours	Europe	4–6 weeks
Spain	44 hours		
Asia/Latin America	48 hours		

Text 1

The standard working week in Europe and North America is 40 hours, but in both Switzerland and Spain this is higher, at 43 hours and 44 hours respectively. In contrast to this, in Latin America and Asia longer hours of up to 48 hours a week are normal. Workers in North America can expect only 10–20 days of paid vacation, while their European counterparts generally enjoy 4–6 weeks holiday a year.

Note how Text 2 below presents the same information differently.

Text 2

Whereas the average working week in most of Europe and North America is 40 hours a week, in Switzerland and also in Spain a worker can expect to work 3 to 4 hours longer. However, the situation, is quite different in Latin America and Asia, where the working week is usually 48 hours. In Europe the situation with regard to holidays is much better than in the States. For example, in Europe most people have from 4–6 weeks holiday. In contrast, the American workers receive only 10–20 days.

4   From the notes below write a short summary, comparing British middle managers with their French and German counterparts.

    Quality of Management – same in UK, France, Germany.

    Higher salaries for middle managers in France and Germany – three times more.

    Also greater responsibilities and higher status.

    Tax lower in France and Germany.

5   Governments of the left, such as François Mitterand's Socialist government in France, have favoured nationalisation of important industries. Governments of the right, such as the British Conservative government under Margaret Thatcher, have favoured de-nationalisation, or privatisation.

What are the points for and against these strategies, considered from the point of view of:

a   the employees?

b   the national economy?

6   The tables below give some information comparing the performance of US companies and Japanese companies operating in the US.

a   Decide on different ways of joining the information in both tables into one complete text.

b   Write a complete text comparing the information given.

US company	Japanese company based in the USA
TV Company	TV Company
400 employees	400 employees
35% female workforce	35% female workforce
Situated in prosperous suburban area	Situated in prosperous suburban area
High degree of cost control, well-developed computer systems	Changing over to centralised computerised system
New factory, up-to-date production methods and equipment	Modern production facilities and methods
	25% more productive
Airline Company	Airline Company
Use local workforce for ground operations	Use local workforce
Unloading of baggage 35% faster	Average unloading rates
Able to change jet engine 30% faster	

FOCUS ON INTERACTION

Hans Daniel is the Purchasing Manager of a German company. He is planning a week's visit to some engineering companies in the UK, including Bennett Ltd, a London based company. He wants to see their Sales Manager, James Robins. Mr Daniel and Mr Robins met at an exhibition in Frankfurt last year, and he now wants to follow this meeting up and discuss the possibility of placing some orders with the British company.

Telephoning

3

1   Listen to the beginning of this telephone conversation in which Hans Daniel tries to contact James Robins. The receptionist answers.

How does Hans Daniel make his opening request?

What else could he have said?

2 Predict what will happen next. Discuss how you would react in this situation if you were Hans Daniel. Then act out the next stage of the conversation.

 3 Now listen to how Hans Daniel deals with the situation.

How does the receptionist tell Hans Daniel to wait a minute?

What phrase does she use to tell him that he is going to speak to Mr Goodbody?

4 The following phrases were used in the dialogues. Match them with the appropriate category, following the example:

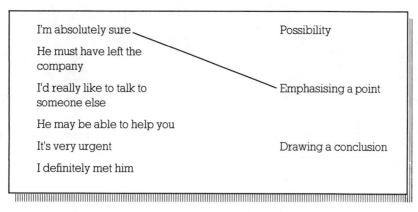

I'm absolutely sure   Possibility

He must have left the company

I'd really like to talk to someone else   Emphasising a point

He may be able to help you

It's very urgent   Drawing a conclusion

I definitely met him

A meeting has been arranged for Mr Daniel to see Mr Goodbody. Bennett Ltd was taken over by TBI about a year ago, and in a major reorganisation, Mr Robins left the company.

Meetings

 5 Listen to the extract from the meeting in which Mr Goodbody explains some of the changes that have been made in the company.

As you listen complete the two diagrams which show the previous and present company organisation.

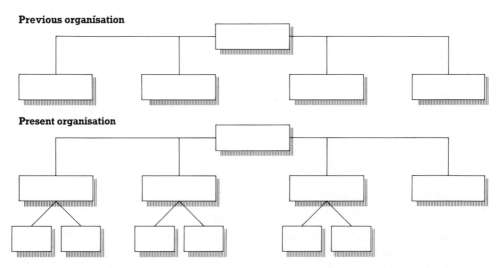

Previous organisation

Present organisation

6   Now listen to the extract again. Pick out any examples of phrases used to emphasise or reduce the strength of what is said:

e.g.   *I'm a little confused.* (reducing the strength)

Socialising   **7**   Listen again to the beginning of the extract, and answer these questions:

a   How does John Goodbody introduce himself?

b   How does Hans Daniel reply?

8   Here are some other ways of introducing and greeting people.

9   Act out the following situations:

a   You have just arrived to visit someone at a company. Introduce yourself at Reception.

b   You are the host at a party. Introduce two guests to each other.

c   You and a colleague arrive from abroad. You are being met at the airport by someone you know. Greet the person and introduce your colleague.

ACTIVITIES

Presentation   **1**   Give a short description of your own company structure, or any other organisation you know.

It should contain the following information:

a   Details of the organisation and how it works.

b   Your own position in the organisation. Who is above you and who is below?

2   Read the following extract from an article about a medium sized engineering company.

There have been considerable changes at Grimes Engineering over the last three years. From a company with problems of declining sales and overmanning, it has developed into a successful exporting company with high productivity. This turn-around was achieved not by reducing activities but by investing in new product lines ...

Join the following items of information together to complete the article. First of all decide which items of information to group together.

Then	*Now*
500 employees	1800 employees
One factory	Three factories
1 Sales Manager	2 Sales Managers
Domestic sales only	International and domestic sales
Little money spent on research	Significant investment in research
Computer used only for internal accounts	Heavy use of computer systems for production and distribution as well as accounts
No overseas offices	Permanent representation in Europe

3   The table below shows some information about the UK. Make a similar chart with details about your country. How would you compare this with the situation in the UK?

United Kingdom

Price of petrol Under 45p a litre in 1984

Housing in London
The cost of a two bedroom flat in London: £30,000–£50,000
Rent: £60–£100 per week

Official Working Week
40 hours. Many office workers work 35 hours a week or less.

Holiday Length 3–5 weeks

Tourism: Destinations in order of popularity France, Spain, Italy, Austria, USA

Average gross income in London

Departmental Manager: £11,000	Bank Clerk: £8,000
Secretary: £7,250	Primary School Teacher: £9,200
Electrical Engineer: £11,200	Unskilled Construction Worker: £6,600

2   A QUESTION OF DELIVERY

LANGUAGE REVIEW: Making polite requests; Stating cause and effect

Making polite requests

*Coronel, a company which produces frozen cakes, is looking
for a new supplier of display materials.*

 1   Listen to the tape and answer the questions below. You
will hear Barbara Hopkins of Coronel telephoning a firm of
printers, Extra Set, to ask for information about cardboard
wrappers, posters and display boards.

a   Is this Coronel's first contact with Extra Set?

b   Barbara Hopkins wants information about:
     wrappers
     posters
     displayboards
How many of each does she want?

c   When does Barbara Hopkins need the information?

d   Why is Coronel changing supplier?

e   When does Barbara Hopkins think they will need to
reorder?

f   Why does Mr Lewis want to arrange a meeting?

Extra Set sample wrapper design

2 Barbara Hopkins makes a number of requests which are summarised below. Listen to the tape again and pick out the phrases which introduce these requests. The first one has been done for you.

Requests	Introductory phrases
for Mr Lewis	Can I speak to … ?
general information about prices	
a firm quote for wrappers	
quote for posters and display stands	
despatch of details by the end of the week	
a quote for reorder of wrappers	

The information below is a letter from Barbara Hopkins to Printal, enquiring about their products.

3a Pick out all the phrases used to introduce requests.

Coronel

The Sales Manager
Printal Ltd
High Rd
Coventry
Warwickshire

12–15 Park Lane
Birmingham

27 February 1984

Dear Sir

We produce frozen cakes and we are looking for a supplier of display packaging and advertising posters.

We would be grateful for firm quotes, with indications of discount allowed, for the following items:

```
250,000 cardboard wrappers - standard size
    500 display boards      - 4 colour
  1,000 display posters      - 4 colour
```

Would you also indicate the probable price if we were to place a firm order in six months and again in twelve months.

It would be helpful to have your reply within the week as the matter is rather urgent and we would like to come to a decision as soon as possible.

We look forward to receiving your reply, including the requested information.

Yours faithfully,

Barbara Hopkins
Marketing Manager

b What is the function or purpose of each paragraph in the letter? Match each of the following functions with the appropriate paragraph.

Identifying your company

Requesting a reply

Closing the letter

Stating the main request

Stating a second request

c Answer the following questions about the language used in the letter:

Why does the letter begin *Dear Sir* and end *Yours faithfully*? What other forms are commonly used and when?

How else could you write the paragraph: *We look forward...?*

4 Draft a letter from Ms Hopkins to Sealite, a company which produces a range of products for sealing foodstuffs. You are interested in Cellefilm wrapping and want to know the price for 2,000 rolls now, and for a repeat order in six months.

5 Request information to complete the chart below, which relates to quotes from the two printing companies.

Extra Set	Printal
Prices for	Prices for
Posters: 1000	Posters: 1000
Display cardboards: 500	Display cardboards 500
Wrappers: 250,000	Wrappers: 250,000
Discount	Discount
Delivery date	Delivery date
Price for reorder of wrappers in 6 months in 12 months	Price for reorder of wrappers in 6 months in 12 months

Printal sample wrapper design

6 On the basis of the information and the samples on pages 12 and 14, decide which company to choose.

7 Use the two situations outlined below as the basis for a telephone call between Coronel and the company you have chosen to supply the order.

a You now wish to order 500,000 wrappers immediately rather than in six months. Same delivery date.

b You have received the design. Request another meeting to talk about some details that you are not happy about.

Stating cause and effect

Mendit, a company which manufactures and distributes kitchen appliances, has been losing sales to its competitors over the last few years, and is trying to identify the reasons for its poor performance.

1 Look at the two diagrams below which show:
the procedure for processing of orders
the procedure for obtaining stock

Identify any weaknesses in these procedures, and then explain how they may have contributed to the company's present problems.

Procedure for processing of orders

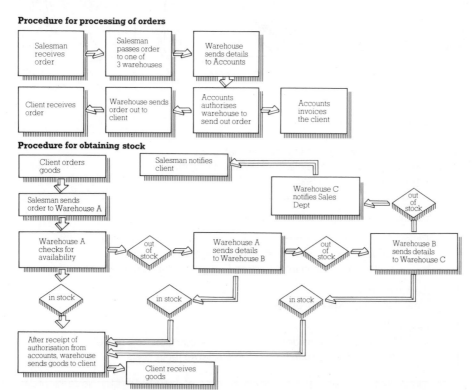

Procedure for obtaining stock

2 Listen to the following extract from a conversation between two people about rearranging a meeting. As you listen complete the following extract from the conversation. Notice the phrases used to describe the reason or cause, and the result or effect of things.

B ... 'the New Marketing Director is descending on us next week ... all the Department Heads have to be here from Tuesday afternoon for a couple of days ... that makes it impossible for me, I'm afraid.

C Is this ... the problem in France?

B It's something to do with that, I think. But the real ... is probably connected with this new distribution system.'

3 Look at the cartoons below. Interpret them and explain the situation. Try to vary the way of presenting the information.

4 The notes below describe the sales situation for domestic appliances in a large electrical company. Connect them to produce a complete text.

Sales of domestic appliances are not as good as before.

Reason
a Production costs in Western Europe are high
b Greater competition from Eastern Europe e.g. for refrigerators and freezers

Additional result
More difficult to export overseas.

Reason
a Many countries outside Europe now produce their own models.
b These models are cheaper. *Reason:* Low labour costs.

---

5   Think of a problem or difficult situation you have been involved in at work. It could be:

> an administrative or technical problem
>
> a difficult situation involving personal conflicts
>
> a breakdown in organisation or procedure

Use the model below to help organise your ideas and then describe the situation or problem.

Give the main details of the problem $\longrightarrow$ Explain why it happened $\longrightarrow$ Show the effects

LANGUAGE STUDY: Analysing cause; Showing a series of consequences

Analysing cause

1   Read the following extract from a report by a Management Consultant. It analyses the causes of a breakdown in the distribution system of a company. Answer the questions in the right hand margin.

Background
Twelve months ago the company had a decentralised distribution system using regional warehouses to supply customers nationwide. However, this system proved to be expensive due to the fact that too much stock was required in each warehouse and large amounts of capital were tied up. As a result, the company began to experience severe cash flow problems.

> What was the original distribution system?
> Why did they change it?

Changes in the Distribution System
The company, therefore, decided to replace the regional warehouses with one central warehouse. All orders throughout the country would be serviced from this central warehouse. This would mean that stock levels could be kept lower, and money would be saved. The new central warehouse would be fully computerised.

> What was the new distribution system?
>
> What were the advantages?

The New Computer System
It took 2 years to design and install the new system. It consisted of a full stock control and order processing system together with a fully automated system for speedy location of goods in the large central warehouse. Due to poor planning the transition period from regional warehouses to one central warehouse was too short and correct procedures for operating the new system were not fully understood. This meant that salesmen did not know how to find out what was in stock and therefore could not inform their customers. This meant a gap of 24 hours between any request for information on stock levels and the receipt of up-to-date information.

> Why did the system begin to go wrong?

The Problem
The regional warehouses were closed down before the new central warehouse was in full operation. Stock that was placed in the new warehouse mysteriously disappeared as it was not entered properly on the computer system. As a result of the inadequate record of stock levels there were huge delays in supplying customers.

> Why didn't the new warehouse have sufficient stock for all orders?

2   Look at the notes below. Analyse the reasons for the breakdown in the system.

Look particularly at the words which indicate explanations or results. These words are in **bold type.**

Effect/Result	Reason	
The original regional distribution system was expensive	Stock levels were too high	The system was expensive **due to the fact that** stock levels were too high.
The company experienced cash flow problems	Large amounts of cash were tied up	… large amounts of capital were tied up. **As a result** the company began to experience severe cash flow problems.
The transition period from four regional warehouses to one central one was too short	Poor planning	**Due to** poor planning the transition period from four regional warehouses to one central warehouse was too short.
Stock disappeared mysteriously	Stock was not entered properly in the computer system	Stock that was placed in the new warehouse mysteriously disappeared **as** it was not entered properly in the computer system.
Huge delays	Inadequate stock records	**As a result of** inadequate stock records there were delays in supplying customers.

3   Match the information in the two columns below, and link the ideas using one of the following words and phrases:

because (of)	due to	therefore
due to the fact that	as	for this reason
as a result (of)	so	consequently

e.g.   *The cost of living is still rising due to the high level of inflation.*

Effect	Cause
The cost of living is still rising	The bank rate is still rather high
Domestic car sales are not as high	Cheap imports from countries such as Korea
The European steel industry is in trouble	Many people are afraid of the unemployment queue
The number of strikes in Great Britain is down on last year	The high level of inflation
Many small businesses are finding it more and more difficult to survive	Japanese competition

Cause	Effect
Oil demand is not very strong at the moment	There has been an increase in the number of people applying for higher education courses
Many countries have been forced to modernise their production methods in the face of competition	We decided to launch a new advertising campaign
Many young people are finding it more and more difficult to find jobs when they leave school	Oil prices have stopped rising
Sales failed to reach the target	Many workers have been made redundant

4 Look at the list of factors which you should think about when choosing a supplier.

Price	Quality
Service	Flexibility
Relationship between buyer/seller	After sales service

Choose one of the following products and rank the factors in order of importance, explaining your choice.

photocopier	small business computer
fuel oil	plastic bottles for milk
adhesive tape for packing	

5a Read the two telexes and pick out the phrases used to introduce the explanations. The notes on the right indicate the writers intention. Match them with the correct part of the telex.

```
FROM BRUTE CONSTRUCTIONS S A FRANCE
TO SMALLWOOD LTD UK
18 NOV.
REFERENCE BATCH NO 34/X2 - DUE TO BREAKAGE
WE REQUEST URGENT REPLACEMENT.
PLEASE SEND SAME QUANTITY AS BEFORE.
CAREFUL PACKING ESSENTIAL.
OWING TO CUSTOMER DEMAND
IT IS VITAL TO SEND REPLACEMENT
AS SOON AS POSSIBLE.
```

Notes
request
reference to order
need for prompt action

```
FROM BRUTE CONSTRUCTIONS S A FRANCE
TO SMALLWOOD LTD UK
20 NOV.
WE REFER TO YOUR TELEX OF 19 NOV.
DUE TO THE FACT THAT REPLACEMENT WILL
NOT ARRIVE BEFORE THE END OF THE MONTH
WE HAVE TO CANCEL ORDER.
WE REGRET THIS DECISION, BUT
THE ORIGINAL DAMAGE OCCURRED AS
A RESULT OF YOUR PACKING.
```

apology
reference to previous telex
states action

b What information do you think was contained in the telex from Smallwood Ltd?

c Draft a suitable telex. It should contain a reference to previous correspondence, an apology, reasons.

Showing a series of consequences

1   Read the following text. What is the purpose of the phrases in **bold type?**

David Brown has been ordered to take a two month holiday. The background to this is that he started to take on too much work. **This meant that** *he took work home in the evenings and at weekends,* **and so** *he had less time for his family and his private life in general.* **This led to** *family tensions and problems* **which meant** *he was working under considerable stress.* **Consequently** *he became less efficient, and* **this resulted in** *several bad decisions in his department.*

  2   Listen to the explanations on tape of the three situations outlined below. Notice how the speakers develop their argument, and pick out words and phrases which connect the ideas which are presented in note form below. The first one has been done as an example for you.

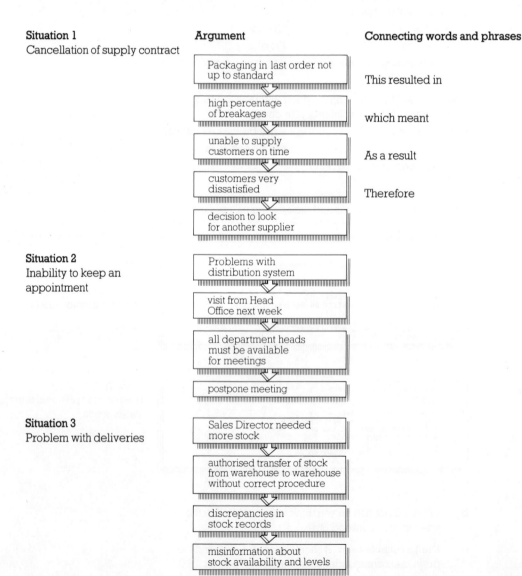

Situation 1
Cancellation of supply contract

Argument

Connecting words and phrases

Packaging in last order not up to standard

This resulted in

high percentage of breakages

which meant

unable to supply customers on time

As a result

customers very dissatisfied

Therefore

decision to look for another supplier

Situation 2
Inability to keep an appointment

Problems with distribution system

visit from Head Office next week

all department heads must be available for meetings

postpone meeting

Situation 3
Problem with deliveries

Sales Director needed more stock

authorised transfer of stock from warehouse to warehouse without correct procedure

discrepancies in stock records

misinformation about stock availability and levels

3　Develop the following statements/decisions with your own detailed arguments.
Give reasons and consequences for each decision.

a　I know it represents a lot of jobs but we'll have to close down our domestic appliances division.

b　It is no good introducing flexitime unless we can include it for everyone, not just the administrative people.

c　Stronger controls should be brought in to protect the European roller bearing industry from cheap imports and dumping by Far East countries.

d　All uncompetitive steel plants should be closed down.

e　The only way to prevent traffic congestion in large cities is to forbid private cars from entering the central area during working hours.

FOCUS ON INTERACTION

SPN UK, one of the subsidiaries of SPN Sweden, produces and sells steel tubes. However, all steel and machinery is supplied from the parent company in Sweden. One of SPN UK's main customers is Endby Tubes.

 9

Peter Maxwell of Endby Tubes is phoning Jim Fox of SPN UK to discuss a delivery problem.

Telephoning　**1**　Answer the following questions:

a　Why is Peter Maxwell calling Jim Fox?

b　How late is the order already?

c　Why can't SPN deliver the steel tubes?

d　Was Mr Maxwell informed about the problem?

e　Why is Mr Maxwell especially worried about this order?

f　What phrase does Mr Maxwell use to introduce himself?
'... Peter Maxwell ... Endby.'
What other phrases could he have used?

g　How does he check the identity of the person he is speaking to?
'... Jim Fox?'

h　Mr Maxwell then states his reason for calling. What does he say?
'... those steel tubes.'
Rephrase the statement using the following:
The reason I'm calling is ...

21

2   The phrases in the left hand column were used in the
dialogue. Match them with the appropriate category on the
right, following the example.

I really am sorry	Makes a strong request
I need to know when we can expect a final delivery date	
I'm afraid we can't say exactly when the machine will be back in operation	Apologises
I've got to know when you can let me have our tubes	Reassures
We're doing everything we can	Makes promises
I can assure you you'll be the first to get the tubes	
I'll look into it and get back to you tomorrow	Demands an explanation
I want to know why we didn't receive that letter	

3   How would you describe Mr Maxwell's attitude in this
telephone call?

Is he angry?
     sarcastic?
     businesslike?
     calm and relaxed?
     critical?

Pick out any example of the language which supports your
view.

4   What should Mr Fox do to pacify Endby Tubes and
make sure he gets his delivery?

5   Is anybody to blame for this situation?
If so, give your reasons.

10 *Later that day Mr Fox calls Mr Palme, the Managing Director
of SPN in Sweden to complain about the late delivery of the
milling machine.*

6   Answer the following questions:

a   What exactly is Mr Fox complaining about?

b   Why can't SPN look for a new supplier for machines?

c   When was the milling machine despatched? Why hasn't
it arrived yet?

d   Who does Mr Palme think is to blame and why?

e   Why does Mr Palme want to send an engineer over to
check the old machine?

7 The phrases below were used in the dialogue by Mr Palme. They are all examples of strong criticism. Make a special note of the stress and intonation he uses.

Surely you realised beforehand that something like this was going to happen

It's really not good enough

You must have realised the machine was in bad shape

You should have reacted sooner

Personally I think you acted too late

8 Find words or phrases in the extract which mean:

a send an order

b almost

c before

d to have a problem with customers

e the machine wasn't in good condition

ACTIVITIES

11   *Jane Newman is a salesperson for a company which produces freezer bags. She is telephoning to arrange a visit to a potential customer.*

Telephoning **1** Listen to the tape and answer the following questions.

a Do you think Jane Newman will be successful in:
   arranging the visit?
   securing the order?
   Give your reasons.

b How would you react if you were Mr Jones?

c What mistakes did Jane Newman make?

d Do you think she is an effective salesperson?

2   Look at the list below. Say which points are important for a good salesperson. Choose the six most important and rank them in order. Then present your findings and explain your choice.

self confidence	tact
enthusiasm	charisma
methodical worker	reliability
smart appearance	good talker
forceful manner	good product knowledge
good telephone style	perseverance
sense of humour	initiative
ability to handle people	special sales training

Are different qualities required for selling industrial and consumer products? If so, what are the differences?

Telephoning   **3**   Act out two telephone conversations, complaining about delivery delays and price changes.

The information is in the Teaching Guide.

Report writing 4   *In 1983 Super Deco, a company which produces a range of wallpapers and paints, found it necessary to look for a new market for its products. Three potential markets were investigated: Europe, the Far East and the Gulf. The chart below summarises the conclusions of this investigation.*

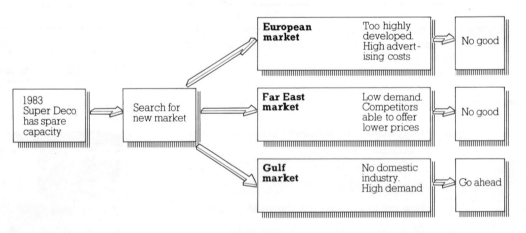

Write a report explaining the company's situation in 1983 and its decision regarding the three potential markets.

Your report should:

PARAGRAPH 1   describe this company's situation in 1983 and consequent decision.

PARAGRAPH 2   define the limits of the investigation which was carried out.

PARAGRAPH 3   present the results of the investigation in:
a Europe and the Far East
b the Gulf

3   A QUESTION OF CONTROL

LANGUAGE REVIEW: Describing present activity; Comparing the past and the present

Describing present activity

1   Below are several pieces of information about the activities of United States Motors (USM). Work in groups, and say which of these facts or activities are **true most, or all, of the time**; which of them are **happening now**; which of them are **not happening now, but may happen**.

a	American technology is the same as Japanese technology, but the management is worse.
b	USM is testing a new system of production.
c	When the factories are operating at full production, unemployment in the Detroit area is much lower.
d	USM is producing compact cars less profitably than the Japanese.
e	The company produces a wide range of cars.
f	When production is operating at full strength, the company employs more than 300,000 people.
g	The company is now suffering the consequences of poor management.
h	The company tests new production systems.
i	The production line is not automated; there are fewer robots than in Japan.

You will hear a representative from USM talking about the company's present position. The extract comes from a television interview.

2 Listen first for general comprehension. Say if the following are true or false:

a The speaker says they are producing faster cars than before.

b The speaker wants to improve production systems.

c It takes the Japanese less than half the time it takes the Americans to produce a compact car

d The Japanese and the Americans are both highly automated.

e The speaker feels quite hopeful about the American position.

3 What words on the tape show that the statements are true? Listen to the tape again, and find the sentences which tell you that these statements are correct. The first has been done as an example.

Notes		Actual words
a	Current production of cars has not changed.	*We are producing cars at the same rate as before.*
b	At the moment the time needed to produce a compact car is very high at USM.	
c	The Japanese can build a compact car more cheaply than USM.	
d	The costs at USM are constantly rising.	
e	The Japanese employ fewer people.	
f	The only solution is to make the control of the production process much better.	

4a Ask other people:
what they do in their job
what special responsibilities they have
what projects/tasks they are working on at the moment

b Write a brief summary of your findings.

Comparing the past and the present

1   Read through the following sentences and agree on their correct order. Organise them so that they make a complete text which gives some background information about Quality Circles. In order to help you, sentences A, D, F, H and J are already numbered.

Quality Circles

   In Europe, Quality Circles are totally different from the system where management and workers are in constant opposition.

F   Those who are involved attempt to solve technical and other problems in an organised way.

H   The supervisors, or foremen, who become leaders of the circle receive training in leadership, and are also trained to present their solutions and suggestions to management.

A   Quality Circles started in Japan, where their objective has been to ensure high product quality, cost effectiveness and punctual delivery, as well as a stable and integrated company workforce.

   The Circle is a small group of people whose task is to discuss problems, and make suggestions which may lead to a solution.

   Quality Circles typically involve people working on the shop floor, that is in the factory.

   It is not a group whose objective is to complain, or to find someone to blame.

J   However, they have been tried with quite a lot of success, and their number is increasing.

   They use brainstorming, diagrams which show the relationship between cause and effect and other procedures which before were only used by management.

D   This type of activity was the fault of many of the old discussion groups which some companies started up in an attempt to solve the differences between workers and management.

2   What are the effects of introducing Quality Circles into a company? List some of the advantages of Quality Circles from the point of view of:

   a production manager

   a line supervisor

   an assembly line worker

13   3   Listen to this extract on tape, in which a machinist, who works on the shop floor of a British company, is talking about certain differences between the past and the present.

As you listen, make a note of the main advantages that he sees about his present situation. Compare this with your list of advantages about Quality Circles.

4   Some statements which refer to what he said are listed below. What sentences does he use which support these statements? The first has been done as an example.

a   There was no variety at work.

The work used to be all the same.

b   He watched the time a lot.

c   In the past he worked only with his hands.

d   Now he thinks as well.

e   In the past, only the management had any ideas.

f   Things were very different in the past.

5   Ask other people about the kinds of things they did in their previous job, that they do not do now.

LANGUAGE STUDY: Recommending and suggesting; Reporting information

Recommending and suggesting

JC Spellman, a food retailing company, has had several years of poor performance. The company has therefore called in a management consultancy to pinpoint the main problems. One of the consultants is giving his findings and recommendations to Arnold Dewar, one of the directors of the company.

14   **1**   Listen to the extract on tape and complete the recommendations below, using the actual words of the consultant.

a   . . . a far better distribution system.

b   . . . you make your first major change here.

c   . . . more depots around the country . . .

d   . . . plan your deliveries a little more carefully.

15   **2**   The following phrases are commonly used when making suggestions and recommendations. Listen to the tape and say whether you think the suggestions are **strong** (confident), or **tentative** (rather careful). Say also if they are **formal** or **informal**.

I wonder if we shouldn't think about it.
I recommend that we start immediately.
We could . . .
My suggestion is that we . . .
What about . . . ? Why don't we . . . ?

3 Suggest ways of solving the following common business problems:

> unequal treatment of women in a company
>
> bad treatment of junior employees by a manager
>
> high costs of office stationery, photocopying and telephoning
>
> poor information about customer needs
>
> higher productivity on the morning shift (06.00–14.00) than on the afternoon shift (14.00–22.00)

4 Write up your recommendations as a list for consideration at a meeting to be held later on.

Reporting information

Arnold Dewar, one of the directors of J C Spellman, is reporting back on the meeting he attended recently with a firm of consultants.
The purpose of the meeting was to brief him on the findings.

16 **1** Listen to the tape and say if the following are true or false:

a The company has a good distribution system.

b The company operates only in a limited area of the country.

c At the moment a large number of lorries go to the shops each day.

d One of the suggestions was to use lorries of the same size.

2 Some actual statements which were made in the meeting are listed below. Listen to the tape again and say how exactly Dewar reports them. The first has been done as an example.

Note: It is very rarely necessary, to report the exact words. Usually, you report *the general idea*.

Original statements	Reported comments
a 'You ought to have a far better distribution system.'	*They said that our entire distribution system needs to be improved.*
b 'You're not competitive because the food isn't fresh enough.'	
c 'You should set up more depots around the country.'	
d 'It's not good to have so many suppliers delivering to the shops.'	
e 'We think you should have the same size lories.'	
f 'When you've got a better system your buyers can look for better quality.'	

3 The following statements relate to the cartoons. However, some of the statements do not accurately report the attitude of the speaker. Write reported statements of your own which are more appropriate.

He asked me if I wouldn't mind sending him the money.

He suggested that Jones might like to look for another job.

He said that we could improve on the quality of our food.

Jones you're fired

This is the worst meal I've had in my life

Send the money at once or I'll call my lawyer!

4 Here are some reported statements. Decide what you think the person really said.

a He advised us to introduce more automation.

b She told us that the price would probably drop during the next 24 hours.

c They said that the cost per unit was ten times higher in America.

d They very strongly recommended that we reduce our operation costs.

e She was quite certain that the right tests had been carried out.

f They warned us not to put the product on the market until it had been properly tested.

g They said that if we did not take the product off the market immediately then they would take us to court.

h He suggested that they froze all wages for at least 12 months.

i They wondered if the problem wasn't caused by too much lead in the product.

17 **5** The two memos below were written following phone calls. Compare the original messages on tape with the written memos. Rewrite the memos if necessary.

a
```
Bob Vincent phoned to say he
wanted 13 boxes on Tuesday.   He
also mentioned that they should
arrive in the morning.
```

b
```
Jim Taylor phoned.   Could you
let him have the figures?   He
seems to think we're not getting
them to him fast enough.
```

FOCUS ON INTERACTION

Carrs produces health drinks. It has a large market in Europe. Paul Jameson, one of the directors of Carrs, has just received a phone call from one of their German clients, a large supermarket chain.

 1 Listen to their conversation and identify the problem. Then decide what Jameson should do.

Memos **2** Read the following memo, from Paul Jameson to Derek Peterson, who works in the company's Quality Control Department. Hobson, a bottling company, supplies them with bottles.

> Derek,
> Hobson have let us down again! We've had complaints in from Germany about fermentation in the bottles. Could you get down to Hobson tomorrow and then come and see me as soon as you get back. *Paul.*

Fermentation occurs when there is bacteria in the water. How do you think this might have happened?

3 Read the following note from Dick Worrall, an assistant in the Production Department at Hobson, to Joe Bright, the Production Manager.

> Joe
> I've just discovered that there's something wrong with the water bottling line. I think we will need to shut the whole thing down and clear the system. My guess is it's the fault of the firm that cleaned the pipes. Shall I get on to them before we start getting complaints? *Dick Worrall*

Derek Peterson phones Hobson. He speaks to someone in their Production Department.

Telephoning **4** Act out the call, explaining the problem and say that you want to arrange a meeting the next day to find out what has happened.

Meetings **5** Now listen to this extract from a meeting between
 Derek Peterson and Paul Jameson. Peterson has already been to Hobson, and he is reporting back.

a Jameson says: '*You didn't believe all that rubbish about the cleaning firm, did you?*'
How is this different to: Did you believe all that rubbish about the cleaning firm?

b   What is the general effect of a negative in questions?
For example: You didn't do it, did you?
You won't come, will you?

c   Jameson shows he is pleased with Peterson. What does he say?

d   When Jameson says: '*What was it?*' what does he mean?

e   Peterson says: '*The same goes for the production line.*'
Express the same idea in a different way.

f   The following verbs are used in the conversation:
set up   get at   sort out
What other verbs have the same meaning?

g   Peterson reports back what he said, and he also reports back the reactions from Worrall and Bright.
Note down what he said.
Note down the reactions.

h   What is Jameson's reaction to Bright's suggestion? What do the words, and the intonation, show?

Letters   **6**   Read the following letter from the Managing Director of Hobson to Paul Jameson of Carrs.

Dear Mr Jameson,

I understand that you have received complaints from Germany about fermentation in your bottles. As you know, this happened before and we found it was due to sub-standard conditions in our water pipes. We have set up very strict controls at Hobson and, considering the huge volume of business, have received very few complaints since then.

The condition of our pipes is looked after by another company, and I am afraid that they are very much to blame for what has happened. Naturally, we apologise and hope that this incident will not cause any problems between us.

Meanwhile, I am sure you will be pleased to hear that we have thoroughly cleaned the pipes and warned the company responsible for cleaning them that we can no longer tolerate such a poor service.

Yours sincerely

---

a   How does Boxer try to maintain good relations between Hobson and Carrs?

b   What placatory phrases does he use?

c   Now write a reply to Mr Boxer, pointing out that you think his company is responsible.

Telephoning   **7**   Act out a phone call between Jameson and Schmidt in Cologne, in which Jameson explains what has happened. Jameson apologises for the problem but does not accept full responsibility. Schmidt is not too happy about this.

Summarising   **8**   Summarise exactly what has happened and the views and opinions of the men involved.

A large supermarket chain is receiving customer complaints about cans of fruit. The fruit has a bad smell. The supermarket chain contacts its suppliers, Frutas de Valencia SA in Spain and calls them to an urgent meeting. The supermarket is particularly worried because it has just signed a large contract with the Spanish company for the delivery of a large quantity of tinned goods over the next two years. Before the contract was signed, a delegation from the Supermarket visited Valencia, and the Spanish company guaranteed to establish a well coordinated Quality Control Department.

Present at the meeting are:

Supermarket chain:
Purchasing Manager
Quality Control Manager
One of the Directors

Frutas de Valencia SA:
UK Representative
International Marketing Manager
One of the Directors

First, each faction in the meeting – the Supermarket chain and Frutas de Valencia – should meet together to discuss their respective positions. Then the full meeting should be held. Full details are in the Teaching Guide.

General information

UK Supermarket chain

- More than 350 + branches throughout the UK.

- Last year's pre tax profit: £65m.

- Has UK and overseas suppliers for a wide range of consumer products.

- Sells Frutas products under Frutas and own brand labels in all outlets.

Frutas

- Supermarket is now 20% of Frutas turnover in UK.

- Has its own warehouse at Bristol (UK port of entry). Now has on-line communications with the six regional supermarket warehouses.

- Frutas receives orders from the supermarket, and then distributes directly to the regional warehouses of the supermarket. The supermarket then distributes directly from each regional warehouse to the branches.

- Frutas has established an excellent costs saving distribution system which enables it to sell very competitively.

- No previous contract with the supermarket, but previous business.

- Made with Frutas for 2 years. The contract has been running for 6 months.

- Frutas to supply 12 lines vegetables
  10 lines fruit
  8 lines fruit juice
  + fresh fruits

These are subject to change at the supermarket's discretion.

- Frutas to guarantee all deliveries, subject to penalty.

- Fixed purchase price for 12 months, with maximum 5% increase in second year, subject to negotiation.

- The Spanish company accepts UK legislation, and guarantees to reimburse for all unaccepted goods.

4   A QUESTION OF CAREER

LANGUAGE REVIEW: Describing changes; Future developments

Describing changes

1   Below you will find several pieces of information about John French's career. However, they are not in the right order. Reorganise the information and present it in the correct sequence to the rest of your group.

> September 1969 – February 1971: Travelled overseas
>
> September 1966: Began 2 year course in Food Sciences
>
> March 1971: Joined Cola Beverages Quality Control Dept. as Laboratory Analyst
>
> July 1966: Left Agricultural College
>
> September – December 1983: Took financial and economics training courses at HQ Amsterdam
>
> 1972: Promoted to Head of Laboratories
>
> December 1982: Cola taken over by Panta
>
> September 1983: Became Head of new Production Control Dept.
>
> 1978: Appointed Head of Quality Control

20   2   Now listen to the interview which John French gives for the company paper.

a   Pick out any words or expressions which show the relationship *in time* between the different events mentioned in the notes:
e.g. *You were with Cola **before** Panta took over.*

b   Are there any other 'time' words or expressions which could be used?

3 Look at the different time expressions below, some of which are used in the interview.

before that	afterwards	subsequently
soon after that	3 years before that	not long after that
prior to that	immediately before	previously
a few years later	sometime later	following that

Using the time chart below, decide which side of the definite point in the past these phrases belong to. The first two have been done as examples:

1978 Became Head of Quality Control

Before that	Definite point	After that

4 *The notes below refer to SABRE, a company which produced cassette recorders and record players. It went into liquidation in September, 1983.*

Before	1982 Launch of K 343	After
1977–82: slow deterioration of market position		1982–3: fall in sales 1983 April: reported heavy losses 1983 September: collapse of SABRE

a Write a short account of SABRE's decline.

b Read the article that follows and notice the order in which the information is presented.

c Pick out the time expressions that are used.

Shock news came last week as **SABRE**, one of the major producers of record players and cassette recorders went into liquidation. The collapse of **SABRE** caused great surprise throughout the business and financial world, and is all the more surprising as it follows the launch in 1982 of a new model K343, a cassette recorder with front loading. Unfortunately it came too late. SABRE's competitors were already on the market with high technology models and sophisticated designs. In the five years prior to the launch, their market position had been slowly deteriorating. The company's management refused to face up to the need for new models which reflected the latest technology and design features. Before accepting this need for change SABRE felt that it could rely on its past reputation and quality.

After finally launching the K343, the company did not reach its expected sales forecast. The following year the company recorded a major loss and 6 months later went into liquidation.

Note how in written English the following pattern is used:

Before the company accepted this need for change . . .
Before accepting this need for change . . .

After the company launched the K343 . . .
After launching the K343 . . .

5   You will receive one or more pieces of information about the career of Janet Smith.

Each of the boxes below represents an important event in her life. Complete the chart by asking questions. Further information is in the Teaching Guide.

Month	Year		Month	Year		Month	Year		Month	Year

Month	Year		Month	Year

Future developments

The extract below is from a confidential memo from the Head of Personnel in Amsterdam to the Personnel Manager of Panta UK, about Mr French's future career with Panta.

1   Read the extract and decide if the company's arrangements and plans listed below are **fixed**, **not yet fixed** or only **state** the company's **preference.**

As you know, in four years' time Frank Lewis, Production Director at our factory in Reading, is going to retire. We want John French to take over from him. However, before he takes over we feel he must have more operational experience. In order to give him this necessary experience we have developed a four year career programme for him which we would like you to consider.

First we plan to send him to our factory in Amsterdam, for a period of a year, to gain up-to-date experience of production and quality control methods. Following this we are going to send him overseas for a period of up to three years. This is in line with company policy for all our potential top management candidates. We are thinking of sending him either to Nigeria or to one of our subsidiaries in Singapore. Finally, he will work side by side with the outgoing Production Director, Mr Lewis, for a period of three to six months.

Arrangements/plans

The retirement of Mr Lewis in 4 years

Mr French's appointment in his place

An initial period in Amsterdam

A period working overseas of about 3 years

A posting to Nigeria

A posting to Singapore

A period working side by side with Mr Lewis before he retires

John French is talking informally to a friend of his from another company about how he sees his future at Panta.

2 Try to decide if the various plans and arrangements he mentions are **fixed**, **not fixed yet**, or merely show his **preferences**.

3 Discuss the differences between the way the company sees John French's future development in the company and how he, himself, sees his future.

Identify any potential point of conflict.

4 The expressions below are used by the company and John French to discuss future developments. In each case some words are missing. Complete the sentences and then categorise them according to the criteria: **fixed**, **not fixed**, **preference** as in the example:

e.g. Frank Lewis *is going to* retire (fixed)

We ... John French to take over from him

We ... send him to our factory in Amsterdam

We ... send him overseas, in line with company policy

We ... sending him to either Nigeria or Singapore

He ... side by side with the outgoing Production Director

I ... take over from him as Production Director

I ... that the company ... give me the chance to get the experience I need

My wife ... start full-time work again

She ... do a course in journalism

My son ... start secondary school

5 Ask another person for information about his/her future plans and preferences. Consider both personal and professional aspects.

6 Write a short summary of what you have found out about other people's plans. Use some of the verb forms in **4** above to indicate whether there plans are **fixed**, **not yet fixed**, or only **state preferences**.

LANGUAGE STUDY: Presenting advantages and disadvantages; Stating priority

Presenting advantages and disadvantages

1   What are the advantages and disadvantages of overseas postings from the employee's point of view?

2a   Read the extract from a letter written by a woman who spent some time working in Oslo, Norway.

> The first few months were quite difficult. I didn't have much knowledge of Norwegian when I arrived, and although it wasn't necessary to be a fluent speaker, it certainly helped a lot for everyday life. I never did get used to Norwegian working hours. Starting work at seven a.m. in summer is bearable, but starting at seven in winter was anti-social. The climate came as rather a shock too. The winters were colder than I expected. However, the houses and public buildings were well heated and insulated. December and January were really gloomy months, with only about six hours of daylight but in spite of this there always seemed to be plenty to do, especially once the skiing season was under way.

b   Now look at the notes below and notice the words in **bold type** which connect the ideas.

She didn't need to speak Norwegian fluently	+ Speaking Norwegian helped in everyday life	→	**Although** she didn't need to speak Norwegian fluently it certainly helped a lot.
She found starting work at 7.00 in summer bearable	+ She found starting work at 7.00 in winter anti-social	→	Starting work at 7.00 in summer was bearable, **but** starting at 7.00 in winter was anti-social.
The winters were colder than she expected	+ Most public buildings were well heated and insulated	→	The winters were colder than she expected. **However**, most public buildings were well heated.
There were only about 6 hours daylight in December and January	+ There always seemed plenty to do	→	**In spite of** the short winter days there was always plenty to do.

39

John French is talking to the wife of a colleague of his, who has just spent two years in Singapore.

3   Listen to their conversation, and note any advantages and disadvantages mentioned about the following aspects of life overseas:

Climate

Accommodation

Social facilities

Cost of living

Education facilities

Then be prepared to summarise the information.

The notes below contain information about living conditions for people working in Lagos, Nigeria.

4a   Decide how and in which order to present the information.

b   Join the information to form a complete text. Your text should contain:

An introductory paragraph

Paragraphs on Climate, Accommodation, Medical care, Education facilities, Living conditions

Cars are absolutely necessary for daily life and petrol is very cheap.

Terrible traffic jams in Lagos.

Three months waiting list for primary schools.

Constant shortages of the following:

canned/frozen goods

petrol

Shortages because of distribution problems.

Frequent electricity cuts.

The climate is generally very hot and humid.

Most fresh goods available in supermarkets or in markets.

Health and medical facilities not reliable, even in the major cities.

Necessary to take health precautions, e.g. boil all water.

Accommodation expensive and sometimes difficult to find.

Accommodation in better parts of Lagos well equipped with standard domestic appliances, e.g. fridge, TV, etc.

Hospitals/doctors very expensive.

There are a number of international primary schools. Fewer secondary schools.

John French has been asked to consider a posting to either Nigeria or Singapore.

5a The charts below give some details about the two jobs, about John's family, and about Lagos and Singapore.

Ask questions to obtain any extra information that is missing. Extra information is in the Teaching Guide. Then use all the information you have about the countries, the jobs and his family to decide which posting would suit him and his wife.

Job Description

Country	Singapore	Nigeria
Title		Production Manager
Main responsibility	Re-organise the production facilities	
Some details about the factory	15 years old. Some machinery needs replacing	
Staff		150
Conditions Salary: Contract length: End of contract bonus: Leave and paid travel: Accommodation:		

Personal Information

Status	Married	
Wife	Maribel.	
Leisure interests		
Age	John: 37 Maribel:	
Children		
Other details	Wife a non-driver. Dislikes very hot temperatures. No previous residency abroad.	

b Present your conclusions. Look at all the pros and cons, and give reasons for your decision.

Stating priority

Now listen to Mr Smart, who has just returned from a job in Tuwati. He is talking to a visiting member of his company's personnel department about his experiences.

1   Some extracts from his talk, where he gives advice to the company about what to do for future expatriates, are given below. Complete the sentences.

a   'You ... give them a basic language course.'

b   'You ... give them better briefings about cultural differences.'

c   'You ... warn people about the climate.'

d   'People ... to have more detailed information about schooling.'

e   'People ... to be given more information about the political situation.'

f   '... to meet people who have lived in Tuwati before arrival.'

2   Below is a list of things a company might organise before sending someone overseas. Rank them from 1–7 in terms of importance. Then say which you feel are **absolutely necessary, important, helpful**

Teach the person the language
Organise a preliminary visit to the country
Offer the family 30 hours language training
Send the person on a cross-cultural orientation course
Organise a brief orientation course for the family
Organise additional meetings with nationals of that country
Organise meetings with company personnel who have recently returned

3   Choose one of the following tasks. List the steps necessary to complete the task. Rank the steps you have chosen in order of importance and present them with your reasons.

Computerising the stock records of a company.
Setting up a distribution system in another country.
Moving abroad for three or four years.
Planning an advertising campaign.
Re-locating an office.
Attending an overseas trade fair.
Reorganising a production area.
Setting up new computer systems.

FOCUS ON INTERACTION

You will hear an extract from a meeting between Jim Masters, the Vice President of Panta, John French and the company's Training Manager. They are discussing John French's future posting.

24 **1**   Listen to the tape and answer the following questions.

Meetings   **a**   What are the main details of the company plan for John French?

       b   Why has Nigeria been chosen instead of Singapore?

       c   What is John French's reaction to the two stages of the plan?

     2a   Jim Masters uses an expression which means 'to think about something carefully'. What phrase does he use? Complete the sentence.

         'You've already been told about this, and had a good chance to . . . it . . . .'

       b   He also gives a short summary of their plan for John French.
How does he introduce this?

         'If I . . .'

       c   John French accepts the first stage of the plan.
What exactly does he say?

         'As you know, I'm . . .'

       d   Do you think he accepted this plan immediately?
Which word tells you this?

       e   What descriptive words does Masters use when talking about their plan for John French?

         This . . . new development
Your . . . opportunity
a . . . opportunity
a . . . experience
a . . . chance
a . . . break

         What effect do these words have?

         Can you think of any other descriptive words which could be used to create the same effect?

       f   On two occasions John French tries to explain his position regarding the posting to Nigeria.

         What happens each time and why?

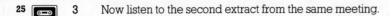

3   Now listen to the second extract from the same meeting.

a   What are the two main arguments that John French uses against going to Lagos?

b   What is the reaction of the other two to these?

c   The Training Manager uses two types of argument to counter French's opposition to his posting to Lagos.
He emphasises the good points of Lagos.
He plays down its bad points.
Find an example of both these tactics.

4   Listen to the tape and complete the phrases below.
What effect do these expressions have? Are they used for:
stressing the importance of some particular action?
emphasising a point of view?

a   '... from the career point of view, it's the best thing for you.'

'... think of my family situation.'

'... I don't really see why the overseas experience is so necessary.'

'It's obvious you can't change company policy. The company says ... go.'

b   What is Jim Masters' last remark?

'So, ... you ... a career for yourself with this company there's ... way.'

What is the effect of this?

5   Look at the situations below and work out arguments that could be used to defend each position. Then act out the situations.

a   The Training Manager meets John French after work and tries to persuade him to accept the posting.

b   The company's Vice President discusses the problem with French's present boss the Production Director. The Vice President strongly believes that French's career prospects will be severely limited if he does not accept the posting. The Production Director emphasises that French is a good manager, and it would not be in the company's interest to lose him.

ACTIVITIES

1 Below you will find a list of factors and personal attributes which may be important in reaching key management jobs.

a Choose six of them and say whether they are **imperative**, **important** or **helpful**. Rank them and be prepared to justify your choice. You may add any other factors which you consider to be very important, but which are not included on the list.

Overseas managerial/work experience

Family support

Willingness to take risks

The ability to change managerial style to suit the occasion

Leadership experience early in career

Special on-the-job training

Wide experience in early career

Self-discipline

Administrative skills

Sound technical training

Drive and initiative

Ability to work with a wide range of people

Ability to negotiate and make deals

b Summarise your results.

2 Look at the table below which shows the advantages and disadvantages, from the company point of view, of sending an employee abroad.

Then join the information to form a complete written text. First of all decide in which order to present the information.

Advantages	Disadvantages
Person loyal to the company	Expensive
Person knows a lot about the parent company organisation	Complex personnel and administrative problems
Person has highly developed skills and experience	Problems of what to do with people returning from overseas
Can be used to train and develop local people	Goes against nationalistic trends of many countries
Greater control of local company	

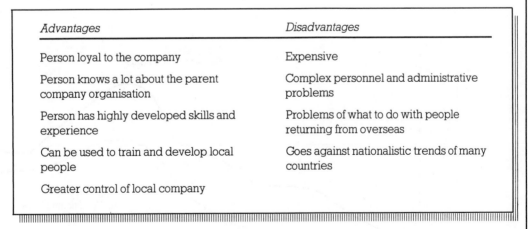

5 A QUESTION OF FUTURE DEVELOPMENTS

LANGUAGE REVIEW: Stating conditions

Stating conditions

IEI produces electrical appliances, particularly air-conditioning units. The company has offices in most of South America, including Dorado, where these units are beginning to sell well. Mr McTavish, the General Manager, is responsible for sales of these units throughout the country.

1   Look through and comment on the graphs, charts and texts below and on page 47. These give information about the economic and political trends in Dorado, and sales of air-conditioning units.

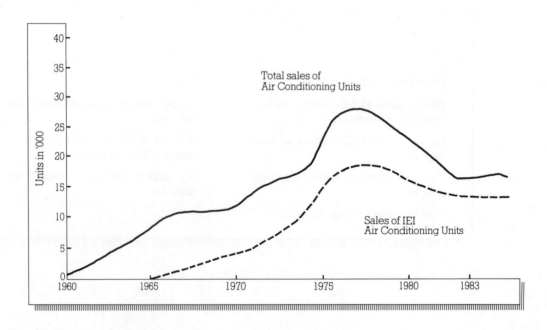

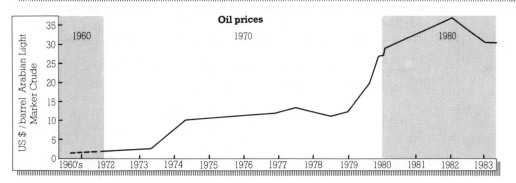

Some Economic Indicators			
	1950	1975	1980
Inflation	—	9%	15%
Growth rate	—	10%	3%
Foreign Exchange reserves	$15m	$400m	$680m
Imports	$200m	$2,400m	$2,150m
Export	$29m	$1,900m	$2,500m
Oil production (barrels per day)	—	250,000b/d	300,000b/d

A decade ago, Dorado lived up to its reputation as a country of political instability and unrest. Governments came and went, and there was no political ideology except the preservation of individual interests. Under the dictatorship of General Diego, despite massive prestigious projects such as the building of the new airport and shipping facilities, the social inequalities persisted and the differences between the 'haves' and the 'have nots' increased. Then in 1979 the socialist UDP won a long and bitterly fought election. Dorado saw a period of stability and massive social programmes made possible by the oil reserves. The question, however, remains: how will declining oil revenues and an insufficient agricultural base affect the newly found political stability?

2   Discuss what you think will happen in Dorado, and in particular to IEI's future sales of air-conditioning units if the following changes occur. Justify your conclusions.

Possible changes

A major international competitor moves into the market.

Local competition increases.

Oil prices don't pick up.

Oil prices harden.

The government collapses.

The influx of people from rural to urban areas continues at the same rate.

The economic and political situation remains constant.

World prices of other exports e.g. bananas and coffee, fall.

Part of the redevelopment programme for Dorado includes the rebuilding of the centre of the capital and the modernisation of some buildings. The government is looking for a supplier of air-conditioning units, and has approached IEI with a contract for 5,000 units worth over £2m.

3   Read the telex from Mr McTavish to headquarters in London and use the information to complete the sentences below.

```
ATTN SALES DEPT
WE NEED 5 000 SK2 URGENTLY.
WE HAVE CHANCE OF MAJOR CONTRACT WITH THE GOVERNMENT
IF WE CAN SUPPLY REQUIRED UNITS AND SPARE PARTS WITHIN
TWO MONTHS.  IF WE DO NOT MEET THIS DEADLINE A.S.S. WILL GET
CONTRACT.  VERY URGENT.  UNLESS WE SUPPLY ORDER WE WILL LOSE
FOOTHOLD IN MARKET.  AWAITING YOUR REPLY SOONEST.

REGARDS  MCTAVISH
```

Condition	Result
If we can supply the required units	. . .
. . .	ASS will get the contract
. . .	we will lose our foothold in the market.

4   Complete the captions for the cartoons.

Unless you improve your appearance I'm afraid . . .

We've no chance of competing, . . .

. . . , unless we get all this computerised soon.

5   Dorado is not a stable country. Certain changes could well occur in the next few months. These changes are listed below. Decide what conditions will produce these changes:

    very high inflation

    overcrowding of the cities

    decrease in the growth rate

    introduction of exchange controls

    return to dictatorship

    increase in defence spending

6 Listen to the beginning of a telephone call from Mr Roberts, head of IEI Sales in London. His first argument and Mr McTavish's reply are summarised in Note **a** below. How would you develop the conversation using the other notes? Act out the situation.

Mr Robert's argument		Mr McTavish's reply
	Worried about the contract. What will happen if . . .	
a	The political situation changes. Reports of instability and a future change of government.	Political situation stable. Government popular, particularly new development plan
b	The economic position changes. Falling revenues from oil.	No problem – getting loan from IMF
c	The government can't get the loan from IMF.	Government very sure about the loan
d	The government can't pay for the contract. What about the 5,000 units?	Impossible to make £2m without risk

LANGUAGE STUDY: Describing trends; Forecasting

Describing trends

27

This is an extract from a presentation given by McTavish to people at HQ in London. He is talking about IEI's business in Dorado.
Below you will find some of the key events which have had a direct or indirect influence on the sales of air-conditioning units in Dorado.

1 Complete the chart, following the example.

Events	Time	Effect on sales positive	negative
Discovery of oil	1960	X	
The first industrial development programme			
Big movement of the rural population to the cities			
Building of major airport and port facilities			
Period of political instability and social unrest			
Election of a socialist government			
Reduction in oil demand and falling oil prices			

Mr McTavish wrote this report following his presentation. The report describes the past performance of IEI and his view of the company's future in Dorado.

2   Complete the notes on the right with any words or expressions which are used to describe upward and downward trends and the rate or degree of the change. Some examples are given.

	Trend	Rate or degree of change

The Early Years

Since IEI opened its first offices in Dorado in 1965, the sales of our air-conditioning units have improved steadily, except for a slight fall towards the end of the 70s. The programme of industrialisation which followed the discovery of oil in the early 60s boosted the construction industry significantly and by the end of the 60s our sales had more than doubled. The capital, Soledad, tripled in size during the early 70s as people flocked to the city in search of work. This led to a significant rise in office and house building, and as a result the demand for air-conditioning units went up noticeably. IEI were well established in the market to benefit from this new and increasing demand.

Trend: improved, a fall
Rate or degree of change: steadily, slight

The Big Boom

In 1973 we were awarded an important contract to supply air-conditioning units for the new airport complex just outside Soledad, and by 1975 our sales stood at 15,000 units. This represented an increase of 100% and established us as market leaders. Sales continued to rise, but more slowly, until 1977.

Political and Economic Uncertainty

Then, in the period 78–80 our sales dropped by 20%, coinciding with a period of social unrest and political change. However our performance was much better than that of our competitors and we maintained our market position.

Political stability returned to Dorado following the election of the socialists in 1979. Unfortunately, government revenues from oil exports fell and this led to a temporary fall in the number of new programmes which had been promised. As a result, our sales decreased by another 20%. At present the government is negotiating a loan with the IMF and it seems probable that we will get new contracts and our sales should recover.

Short Range Forecast

It is always difficult to make predictions in countries where the nature and political colour of the government can change suddenly, but we are fairly confident that the next five years will show a steady increase in IEI's penetration of the market, particularly if the new IMF loan is obtained.

3   Find examples of language in the presentation and
report that could be used to describe the trends in the charts
below.

A

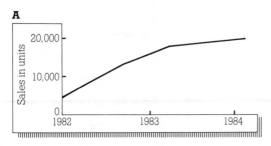

B

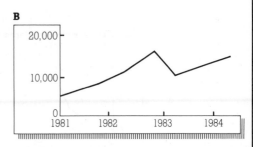

C

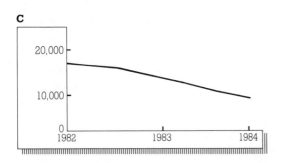

4   Below you will see a graph which shows the
development of the sales of a range of kitchen furniture.
However, it is incomplete.

Ask questions to complete the graph and to identify the key
events which have influenced sales. The necessary
information is in the Teaching Guide.

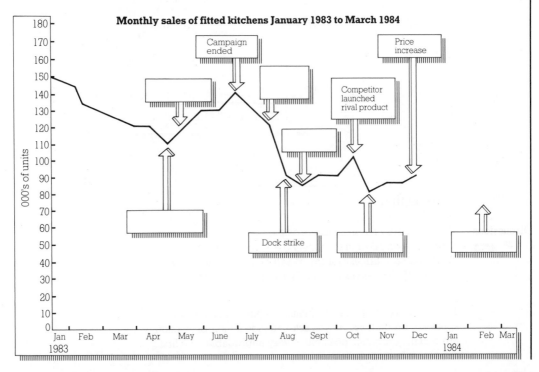

Monthly sales of fitted kitchens January 1983 to March 1984

5   Look at the three charts below. Describe the general trends and highlight any significant influences on these trends.

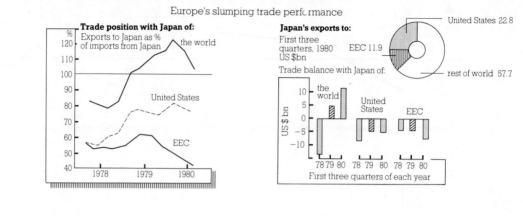

Europe's slumping trade performance

Japan's Motor Cycle Industry

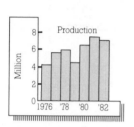

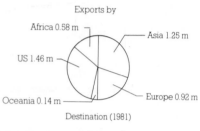

Truck production in leading countries

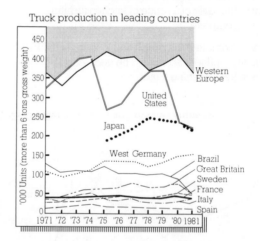

Forecasting

Discussions
28

This is an extract from a debate on the political situation in Dorado. Taking part in the meeting are the interviewer, Enrico Basso, journalist for the socialist paper La Libertad, and Joan Pattern, economic advisor to the US government.

1   The chart on page 53 contains a summary of the two speakers' predictions. As you listen decide if their predictions are **certain**, **probable**, **possible** or **very improbable**. The first ones have been done as an example.

	Prediction	Speaker	
a	No change in policy by government	Enrico Basso	*improbable*
b	Increase in food shortages	Enrico Basso	*certain*
c	More spending on prestigious building projects e.g. new university	Enrico Basso	
d	Possibility of a loan for the government	Joan Pattern	
e	Deterioration of the whole situation in Dorado	Joan Pattern	
f	Government difficulties in fulfilling their election promises	Joan Pattern	
g	Increase in tension in the cities	Joan Pattern	
h	Eventual fall of the government	Joan Pattern	
i	Attempt by the press to turn public opinion against the government	Enrico Basso	
j	Increase in unpopularity of the government	Enrico Basso	

2   The following sentences summarise the predictions made by Enrico Basso and Joan Pattern in the interview. Decide whether these summaries are equal in meaning to what they actually said. If not, say whether they are more certain or less certain than their actual words.

a   It's possible that the government will change its policy.

b   Food shortages will definitely get worse.

c   The prestigious projects will probably continue.

d   The government could find it difficult to fulfil their election promises.

e   Tension in the cities is likely to increase.

f   There's a chance that the press will turn opinion against the government.

3   Make predictions based on the following notes. Agree or disagree with the statements and justify your point of view.
e.g. *Nuclear power/main source of energy/year 2000 (probable)*
Nuclear power is likely to be the main source of energy in the year 2000.

a   Methane gas instead of petrol for cars (possible)

b   Decrease in separatism in next 20 years (improbable)

c   The development of a new international language (possible)

d   Increase in nuclear weapons by USA and USSR (certain)

e   Increase in spending on space programmes (probable)

4   The two sets of notes below give information and make predictions about the impact of new technology on working habits. Connect the notes to produce two separate texts.

a
Word Processors in the Office
Last few years – increase in use of word processors.
Popularity will continue (probable)

Reasons
1   Work less repetitive for the operator
2   Better productivity

Disadvantages
Studies show physical problems (possible)
e.g. eye strain, back problems   (inconclusive evidence)

b
The Factory of the Future
Factory of future look very different (certain)

Examples
1   Increase in the use of robots/automation (certain)
2   Fewer unskilled workers (probable)
3   Smaller production units (possible)
4   Closure of old factories in big cities/move to new industrial zones (probable)

FOCUS ON INTERACTION

1   Read the report below from one of the main daily papers. What are the implications of this report for IEI?

STOP PRESS

News is coming in of a coup in Dorado. At four o'clock this morning a report was received that several army units moved into the capital just before midnight. Early indications are that the government has fallen, and that President Isidoro Macondo has already left the country. At the moment there is no real information about who has taken over, and whether there will be any significant change in the current political and economic policy.

29   *This conversation took place at a party recently held in London for regional sales representatives from IEI. Peter Morgan from London is talking to Tony Hunt.*

Socialising   2a   Listen carefully and answer the following questions:
When did Tony last see Tom McTavish?
Peter tells a story about Tom McTavish. What is it?
What is Tony's explanation for Tom's eccentric behaviour?

b How do you think this conversation will develop? What other topics are likely to be introduced at this stage?

c Act out the conversation as you feel it could develop.

d Describe a funny situation you have experienced.

e Listen to the second part of the tape.
How do you think this news will affect the contract in Dorado?

Several weeks later it becomes apparent that the new government has no intention of honouring many of the old government's contracts, including the one made with IEI. John Roberts from IEI headquarters has flown out to Dorado to see what can be done.

Discussions
30

3 Listen to the conversation between John Roberts and Tom McTavish.

a What has happened about the contract?

b Where are the air-conditioning units at the moment?

c Who does John Roberts think is responsible for the situation?

4 The two men are arguing about who is responsible for IEI's present problems. Listen to the conversation again and complete these extracts.

a John Roberts sees the situation in very negative terms. What two expressions does he use?
'It's ...'
'What ...'

b John Roberts wants to know if it's totally impossible to persuade the government to honour the contract. What questions does he use?
'Are you sure ... we can ... these people ... ?'

c What is Tom McTavish's reply?

d John Roberts thinks Tom McTavish is responsible for the situation. Find any phrases which give you this impression.

e John Roberts is very critical of Tom . What does he say?
'If ... this ...'

f How does Tom McTavish defend himself?
What exactly does he say?
'I really don't see how you ... me ...'

5 Decide what caused this problem for IEI. Is anybody responsible? What do you think should be done?

ACTIVITIES

1   Below you will find a number of points which may affect your company over the next 5 years or so. Discuss any changes you predict in these six areas. Think carefully about whether these changes are certain, probable or just possible.

> Technological developments
> Energy costs
> Political situation
> Employment trends
> Competition from outside
> Raw material availability

2a   Connect the information below into a complete text, using linking words and forecasting phrases. Note the meanings of these symbols:

> +++ certain   ↓ falling
> ++ probable   ↑ rising
> + possible

Situation in UK over the last few years

High unemployment ↑

Inflation ↓

Many small companies closing down ↑

Problems in retail trade. ↑

Industrial action ↓

Forecast for next 5 years

Exports improve ++

Value of sterling against the US dollar ↓ ++

Annual inflation less than 7% ++

Lower wage settlements ++

World economy recover ++

UK balance of trade stronger +

Revenues from oil lower ++

Reasons

Falling world demand for crude oil ++

Interest rates ↓ again ++

More investment in industry ++

Productivity higher +++

Note This information and the predictions are based on the situation in the UK at the beginning of 1984.

---

b   Produce similar information for your country and make a short presentation.

6 A QUESTION OF IMAGE

LANGUAGE REVIEW: Finished and unfinished periods of time;
Hypothetical statements

Finished and unfinished periods of time

1   Think of a recent advertising campaign. Describe it.
Who was it aimed at? Was it successful?

What changes have you noticed in advertising over the last
ten years?

Consider the following:

style

medium (TV, radio, newspapers), etc.

message

Give examples from recent campaigns.

*A senior member of Equity, the actors' union in the UK, is
talking about the problems actors are facing.*

**If an
advertisement
is wrong,
we're here to
put it right.**

The Advertising Standards Authority.✔
ASA Ltd, Brook House, Torrington Place, London WC1E 7HN.

31 [cassette] 2   Listen to the tape. Say whether the following notes refer
to an action or event in the past or an action that is not yet
finished. Note down the actual words used. The first one has
been done as an example.

	Notes	Actual words
a	Earnings from commercials	*Earnings from commercials have always been an essential source of income.*
b	Trend in job prospects for actors	
c	Agreement between IPA and Equity	
d	The start of Channel 4	
e	Commercials with actors on Channel 4	

3   Read this extract from a report on advertising agencies'
use of actors in TV commercials.

A survey of the 15 largest advertising agencies who account for
the bulk of advertising on television, shows that they employed
25% more actors in the first half of last year than they have so
far in the first five months of this year. In the first half of last
year the agencies made 1082 commercials and employed 2752
actors, an average of 2.54 actors per commercial. So far this year
they have made 933 commercials and have used 1784 actors, an
average of 1.91 per commercial. The reason for the drop has
been a steep increase in the level of repeat fees paid to actors.

Now answer these questions:

a   In which period were more actors used?

b   Do both periods cover exactly the same length of time?

c   In which month was this report probably written?

d   When is the past form 'made' used in the extract?
Compare this with the use of 'have made'. Why are both
forms used?

4   A second extract from the same report is written out
below. Where there are two versions of a word or phrase,
choose the correct one.

In 1980 a new agreement **has been reached/was reached** with
the actors' union Equity on the level of payments to actors for
appearances in TV commercials. However since that time
production costs for commercials **have risen/rose** fast, and they
now cost well in excess of £1000 a second to produce. In 1981
alone television production costs **rose/have risen** by 33%. In
addition airtime costs **have also jumped/also jumped**
tremendously. Actors are one of the few controllable factors in
the mix, and many advertisers are now using fewer actors in
commercials, replacing them with cartoons, or with real people
playing themselves.

5   Discuss the following topics with your colleagues.

a   Length of time in a company/department/job

b   Brief history of past and recent work experience

c   Visits to different cities/countries

Hypothetical statements

*Georgia Electronics, an American multinational manufacturer
of computers, calculators, and semi-conductors, with factories
in 14 countries, is planning to change its approach to product
advertising in Europe. Previously it has conducted campaigns
country by country. The new approach is to conduct one
campaign throughout Europe using one advertising agency.*

1   Discuss what this new approach for the company might mean. Talk about the disadvantages and advantages from the point of view of both the parent company and the subsidiaries.

This extract comes from a preliminary meeting about the new approach. The meeting is attended by the Country Managers for Scientific Calculators, the first range of products to receive this new treatment. The meeting is addressed by the European Advertising Manager, Ian Halliday.

2   Answer the following general questions.

a   What are the three reasons for the new approach?

b   What is Dieter, the German Country Manager, worried about?

c   What two concerns does Sven, the Swedish Country Manager, have?

3   The German and Swedish Country Managers were concerned about several hypothetical developments. Listen to the extract again and complete these sentences.

a   If Germany contributed the largest amount to the central advertising budget ... a proportionately large share of the allocated funds?

b   Unless we ... that, it would cause a lot of discontent.

c   What ... we do if there ... a sudden rise in the dollar?

d   If we really wanted to reach ten European countries we ... it in the local languages.

Car advertising is one type of advertising which many people are familiar with. This form of advertising is often used to support and reinforce individual beliefs and prejudices about different makes and models.

4a   Think of a recent advertising campaign for a car. Which of the features listed below were emphasised?
fuel economy
style
price
reliability
speed and acceleration
comfort
size

b   If you wanted to sell a car to the following groups which of the features below would you emphasise, and why?
single young executive
company director
family with young children

Presenting information

The table below shows a list of the UK companies that advertised most heavily in 1980. Discuss any points of interest and significance.

Most heavily advertised brands, 1980 (Press and TV)								
General list					*Excluding retailers*			
		£m	Press (%)	TV (%)			£m	Press (%)	TV (%)
1	Co-Op	8.84	73	27	1	Dulux	4.81	16	84
2	Boots	7.65	69	31	2	Ford Range	4.50	54	46
3	Woolworth	7.39	45	55	3	Midland Bank	4.47	28	72
4	MFI	6.81	85	15	4	Guinness	4.46	13	87
5	Asda	5.63	54	46	5	Vanguard	4.25	100	—
6	Tesco	5.61	87	13	6	Lambert and Butler	4.23	100	—
7	Currys	4.92	88	12	7	Players KS	3.89	100	—
8	Dulux	4.81	16	84	8	British Airways	3.77	33	67
9	Ford Range	4.50	54	46	9	Embassy	3.52	100	—
10	Midland Bank	4.47	28	72	10	Halifax BS	3.48	55	45

Source: MEAL

1   Read this text about the statistics in the chart and answer the questions alongside about the organisation of the information.

Britain's top retailers still dominate the league table of big spending advertisers. Since 1975 at least nine, and usually all ten of the top spots have been occupied by retailers, with **Boots** holding the number one position between 1976 and 1979. **The table above shows** that the domination of the retailers continues, **although** Boots is no longer top and **for the first time** in six years there are three non retailers in the list.

The second section of the table shows the ranking excluding retailers. Comparing the 1980 non-retail list with that of the previous year there are seven newcomers. **Only** Wills Embassy, British Airways and Halifax Building Society have held their places, **but** seven new brands lead the table.

Looking at the Press/TV ratios in the two top ten lists we can divide the brands into three fairly discrete groups. **Firstly**, the cigarette brands which cannot be advertised on TV and so allocate all their expenditure to the Press. **Secondly**, the retailers, who with the single exception of Woolworth use both media but concentrate most of their spending on the Press. **Lastly**, the remaining brands which allocate between 45% and 87% of their spending to TV.

1980 was a boom year for big-spending on advertising, with a leap from 110 to 257 'millionaire brands'. Seventy-three brands spent at least £2m. **The question remains, however,** whether this increase in marketing and advertising budget will continue in the face of the growing recession.

a   What is the function or purpose of the four paragraphs? Choose from the following list. Some paragraphs may have more than one function.

-focusing on one part of the table
-summarising the general trend
-analysing the information
-introducing the topic
-giving background information

b   In what way do the words and phrases in **bold type** help to organise the information or focus the attention of the reader on significant details?

Presentation
33 📼

2   Now listen to a presentation of the same information.

a   Pick out any differences between the spoken and written forms for presenting information.

b Listen for the following phrases and say what their
purpose is:

'Before going on . . . let's look at . . .'

'Of course'

'. . . what's interesting here is'

'In fact'

'First of all we have'

'Then we have'

'That leaves the other brands'

'One final comment'

'. . . so to speak'

'Whether or not they'

c In the presentation find the spoken equivalent of the
following formal phrases from the written text.

The table above shows

. . . dominate

. . . there are (three non-retailers)

The second section of the table shows

Firstly, . . . secondly, . . . lastly . . .

The question remains, however, whether . . .

continue

A good presentation or written report needs to be well
organised, with clear signals to the listener or reader to show
how one idea leads on from another.

3 The table below gives some examples of signals.

a Categorise them according to the separate headings.

b Say if you think they would be used in a written or
spoken text.

c What other signals can you think of for each category?

Categories	Signals
Introducing a topic	What I want to talk about is . . .
	After that . . .
Sequencing of ideas	In the graph we can see . . .
	Let's start by looking at . . .
Reference to visuals	So, to sum up . . .
	Now, I'd like to turn to . . .
Turning to a new topic	I would like to describe/explain/show . . .
	As mentioned above . . .
Returning to a point	There are three main points . . .
	The graph/table shows . . .
Summarising	As I said . . .

4 Look at the following table.

Advertising at Exhibitions and Trade Fairs

Advantages	Disadvantages
1 Prestige	1 Needs very careful organising
2 Localised	2 Inflexible timing
3 Personal contact with potential buyers/customers	3 Inflexible location
4 Suitable for large or complicated products/services	
5 Testing the product/service	

---

a Introduce the topic and indicate the main points to be considered, including the order in which you intend to consider them. Do this in both a spoken and written form.

b Now go on to expand on the points you have introduced, and in particular give explanations or further information.

5 Now take one of the charts or tables below and give a complete short presentation.

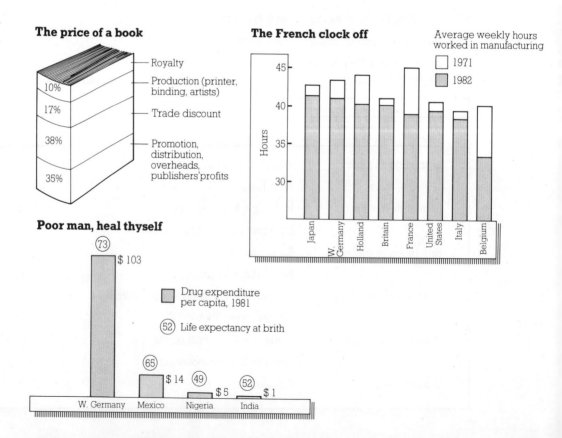

The price of a book

- Royalty
- Production (printer, binding, artists)
- Trade discount
- Promotion, distribution, overheads, publishers' profits

10%
17%
38%
35%

The French clock off

Average weekly hours worked in manufacturing
☐ 1971
▨ 1982

Hours: 45, 40, 35, 30

Japan, W. Germany, Holland, Britain, France, United States, Italy, Belgium

Poor man, heal thyself

▨ Drug expenditure per capita, 1981

(52) Life expectancy at brith

(73) $103 — W. Germany
(65) $14 — Mexico
(49) $5 — Nigeria
(52) $1 — India

Advertising on Television

Advantages		Disadvantages	
1	Combined impact of sight and sound (action)	1	Expensive
2	Geographical flexibility	2	Timing difficult
3	Intimacy of appeal (relaxed)	3	Competing with other activities
4	Prestige	4	Mass audience – non-selective
5	Newsworthy ('did you see x last night?')	5	Must be supported by wide distribution
6	Frequent repetition	6	Expensive to produce

Connecting ideas within sentences

1a What are the objectives of the two advertisements below?

b How are the advertisements different?

2 Read the following extract from a report on corporate advertising in OILCO, a large multinational oil company.

The words in **bold type** are reference words.
What does each one refer to?

The usual application of corporate advertising is to show the size and importance of a company, **its** financial standing, the wide range of **its** products, or even the number of staff **it** employs.

However things are changing. In recent years there has been much criticism of large business, and in particular of those companies **which** operate worldwide i.e. the multinationals. **They** are accused of making too large profits, setting **their** prices too high, of having little concern for the environment, and so on. These factors, **which** have been accompanied by a rapid rise in consumerism, have forced companies into a defensive situation **where they** feel it necessary to explain **their** role in society to the general public.

OILCO is an example of a company **which** has recently turned to corporate advertising as the most effective way of explaining **its** programmes and policies to mass audiences. Much of this advertising has been on television, **which** confirms the company's belief that there is a particular need to put across views to mass audiences. In addition OILCO is using colour pages in the national press, featuring conservation (among other subjects) as the foundation **on which it** can build all **its** other product advertising.

3 Rewrite the following sentences using reference words, following the instructions alongside.

a The exchange rate of the dollar will continue to fluctuate. The exchange rate of the dollar has a direct effect on profit margins in European countries.

Rewrite in one sentence.
Use: which

b Improvement of the plant has to be undertaken. Improvement of the plant will cost nearly 3m US dollars, but 3m US dollars can be borrowed quite easily.

Rewrite in two sentences.
Use: it, this

c Environmental protectionists have made increasing political ground in recent years. Environmental protectionists have a great deal to say about production processes in industry. The involvement of environmental protectionists in industry increases costs greatly.

Rewrite in one sentence.
Use: who, which

d Large businesses are cutting back on costs in administrative areas. Small businesses are cutting back on costs in administrative areas. Administrative areas, in times of profit, tend to grow. However, large businesses and small businesses face the danger of overcutting, especially on the sales and marketing side. Overcutting can have an adverse effect on future margins.

Rewrite in two sentences.
Use: both, which, they, which

4 Choose from the following list to complete the text below and on page 65. Each word or phrase can be used once only, unless otherwise indicated.

which (3)   that (2)   one   it   who   the other   this

The consumer's relationship with his or her car is probably unique. . . . is an expensive high-risk product . . . makes the purchasing decision a very seriously considered one, and one

... the buyer has to live with for some time. The figures for households with more than one car demonstrate the degree to ... people now rely on cars. There are two principal consumer requirements fulfilled by the motor car: ... is functional, ... psychological. The functional benefit is related to the use ... will be made of the car, e.g.: people ... have two large dogs want an estate car; most people with large families want a four door model.

The other function of a car, the fulfilment of a psychological need, usually comes second. There are two aspects to this. Firstly owning a particular make or model is something ... gives personal satisfaction. Secondly it represents a social statement made to others.

FOCUS ON INTERACTION: Argumentation and discussion; Socialising

Argumentation and discussion

In Language Review, *reference was made to the plans of Georgia Electronics to centralise their advertising throughout Europe. This plan clearly met with certain doubts and fears from the national subsidiaries.*

34 *This extract is taken from another meeting of the Country Managers for Scientific Calculators. The meeting is chaired by Ian Halliday, the European Advertising Manager.*

Meetings 1 Answer these questions:

a What is Dieter doubtful about?

b What does John, the UK Country Manager, object to?

c How does Ian end that part of the discussion?

2 Now answer the following more detailed questions about what was said. If necessary listen to the extract again.

a How does Ian introduce his summary? What words does he use?

b Dieter immediately asks a question. Does he want:
more information?
a repetition of what was said because he didn't hear it?
clarification on some point?

c What exactly does he say? Complete the sentence:
'... harmonise the company's image, ... that ...'

d Does Ian confirm or deny what Dieter says? What does he say? What else could he have said?

e Dieter again shows his disagreement with Ian's idea. How does he introduce his argument? Complete the sentence:
'... how you can run the same campaign ...'

f Having stated his point, Dieter then goes on to explain why he believes that the same campaign will not work in different countries. What phrase does he use to introduce this explanation?

g John interrupts Dieter, and disagrees with him. Does he do this politely or impolitely? How do we know? What does he say?

h Dieter immediately interrupts and argues against John's point. His opening phrase indicates that he is going to disagree with John. What is it?

i Ian tries to bring the two to order, and then he summarises the main objectives for the group. How does he introduce this summary? What does he say?

3 Listen to the extract again and find phrases that match the following categories.

interruption	summarising + focusing
request for clarification	agreeing/disagreeing
stating conditions	

4 The script below is from a later stage in the same discussion. It does not appear on the tape. Follow the guidelines on the right to complete the text.

DIETER	Another thing I . . . is the way of funding this project. How can we be sure we'll get the full value of what we contribute?	disagreement
IAN	I think you've missed . . . What we want to do is create a European programme that will benefit everyone in the long run.	focusing on the main point
JOHN	Yes, Dieter, Ian is right. . . . we want to do this on a Europe-wide basis, . . . each individual country will have to make some compromises.	stating the condition for something
DIETER	That's . . . well, but we're still judged on our sales figures at the end of the day. And what exactly . . . by 'compromises'?	continued disagreement asking for explanation
JOHN	I mean we'll all have to work as part of a team, for the common good. That's the . . . of this new project.	stating the main point again
SVEN	Can I just . . . here. I think Dieter is right here. Basically . . . we are sure that our turnover won't be affected, very few of the subsidiaries will be keen to experiment . . . I think we should try to think of another way of financing this whole thing.	interruption stating condition logical conclusion

5 What do you think of this company's decision to centralise their advertising?

Socialising

The various Country Managers of Georgia Electronics are invited out by some of the people at the Head Office, which has recently relocated from Paris to the south of France, near Nice.

35 **1** Listen to the short extracts from the conversation in the restaurant and answer the questions.

Socialising

Extract 1

a What is the topic of this conversation?

b Write down the four questions John asks.

c What particular subjects are discussed?

Extract 2

a Notice that Pierre always gives approximations in his descriptions of the food. How many ways does he do this? What phrases does he use?

b How does he try to describe 'oursins de mer'?

c Sven probably doesn't know what 'oursins de mer' are, even after Pierre's explanation. How does Pierre finish his explanation, indicating that it's unusual?

Extract 3

a How does John bring up the subject of Hamburg? What does he say?

b Why does John say *so* in 'So what should I see ...?'

c What words does Dieter use to describe parts of Hamburg, and the things John should see and do?

d How does John finish this conversation?

2a Make a list of unusual national dishes, then try to explain them to a foreign visitor.

b Suggest to a visitor some things to see and do in the area where you live.

c Someone has just arrived in your town. What would you say in the first few minutes to make him/her feel at ease? Act out the conversation.

Poissons

Demi Langouste
Grillée 50F
Sole Grillée
Sauce Béarnaise 56F50

Plats du Jour

Canard Sauvage
au Poivre Vert 52F
Gras Double à la
lyonnaise 36F 50
Steak Tartare 42F
Côte de Boeuf
78F
Steak Grillée
Maitre d'Hôtel 40F

Grillades

Entrecote Grillée, Beurre Maitre d'Hôtel 53F 50
Chateaubriand 64F 50 Béarnaise 4F 50
Escolope de Veau 40F Pied de Porc Grillée 30F
Légumes   Haricots Verts
Pomm

1   Act out a meeting, similar to the one at Georgia Electronics, in which the advertising policies of a company are being discussed. The company produces calculators, for both personal and business use. The problem is one of coordinating image. The roles are in the Teaching Guide.

You should include the following facts or arguments in the discussion:

The advantages of a new Europe-wide campaign.

The disadvantages as seen by the Country Managers:

> unfair distribution of budget
>
> different national characteristics
>
> problems of co-ordination
>
> lack of independence to choose own advertising approach
>
> possible adverse effect on sales figures on which they are ultimately judged
>
> currency conversion problems (everything quoted in $)

The budget allocated to the campaign by different countries would be something like this:

Sweden	$ 1.0m	Italy	$ 3.0m
Germany	$10.0m	UK	$ 6.0m
Portugal	$ 0.5m	France	$ 5.0m

This represents a percentage of turnover.

2   Corporate advertising can be divided into two types:

Institutional/Image Advertising, which aims to create a specific corporate personality in the mind of the public and customers.

Idea/Issue Advertising, which is more concerned with putting forward ideas about social, environmental issues and the company's position on these. It sets out to show the company as a 'nice guy' that would not pollute the environment or become involved in any kind of corruption.

The table on page 69 shows the range between pure Image advertising and what can be called Advocacy Advertising.

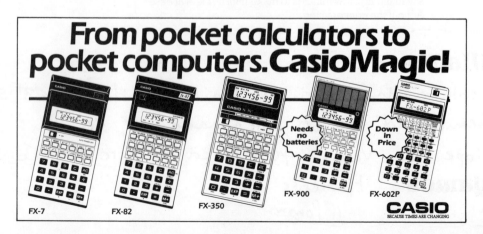

Collect examples of adverts and put them into one of the two categories, and try to rank them on the chart.

A Scheme for Classifying Corporate Communications	
Type of Message	**Description**
Institutional/Image – Goodwill	Message intended primarily to generate goodwill. Carries a minimum of corporate identification.
Institutional/Image – Name Identification	To bring the corporate name and logo to the attention of current and potential customers, suppliers, employees, and investors.
Institutional/Image – Activity Identification	To bring corporate activities to the attention of current and potential customers, suppliers, employees, and investors.
Idea/Issue – Indirect Advocacy	Describes company activities in terms that suggest they serve public interest thereby indirectly advocating these activities as preferred solutions.
Idea/Issue – Direct Advocacy	Advocates a specific viewpoint or approach to problems in society. Includes messages regardless of whether the reader is urged to take a specific action.
Idea/Issue – Disguised Advocacy	The message supposedly presents both sides of the arguments. However, the choice of arguments, relative emphasis, and attention to detail are invariably biased and therefore are a form of subtle advocacy.

3   You are involved in planning an advertising campaign for one of the following. Build up individual presentations comparing the suitability of different media, with their advantages and disadvantages, and suggest the best mix.

a bank's customer services to individuals and small businesses

an airline

a range of kitchen units

a range of cosmetics

a new magazine for women

a micro-computer for personal or small office use

industrial shelving for warehouses

CASE STUDY 1

The right person for the job

The European headquarters of Betatone, a large multinational company producing electronic components, employed two Training Managers. Vera Jones looked after the production of materials specially designed for use on in-company courses and for self instruction. Harold Schumann was responsible for organising and co-ordinating all courses held inside and outside the company. Each manager was responsible to the Personnel Manager, François Trudeau. (See chart below.)

Examples of courses prepared by Vera Jones are on the use of computers, the operation of accounts, and sales and marketing. Harold Schumann organised people to go on the courses prepared by Vera Jones and he also arranged for company employees to attend courses organised by outside training organisations.

For a long time it was felt that the company should have only one Training Manager, who would co-ordinate all training activities. Vera Jones had been with the company for ten years and was the obvious candidate. However, Harold Schumann did not share this opinion. In his view Vera Jones was not the person for the job. He felt her ideas and techniques were out of date.

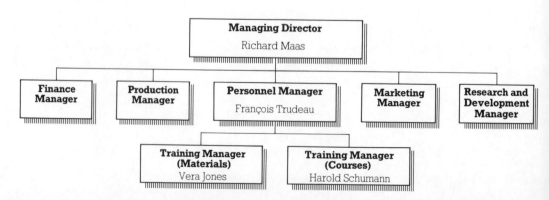

1   Read the following extract from a memo, written by
Vera Jones to Richard Maas, the Managing Director of the
company.

Date: 23rd June, 1983

To: Richard Maas   From: Vera Jones
      Managing Director   Training Manager (Courses)

Subject: Special Courses   Confidential

For some time it has been apparent that the existence of two managers
within the training department has not been in the best interests of
the company.   Now that a decision is to be taken by the board to
correct this position I feel I should write to you briefly to express
my feelings on the matter.

Clearly there will be a choice made between myself and Harold Schumann.
In the final event, one of us will be forced to leave the company, or
at best be transferred to another department. Neither of these in my
opinion, would reflect the hard work I have put into the development
of in-company training and the very high standard of the courses themselves. I will not list the packages and programmes which I have
initiated, as these are well known to you, but I will say that of the
two of us I am the only one with experience in the development of
courses. Harold Schumann is an administrator, a very good administrator, but he has not, in the four years he has spent with us, ever
supervised the development of any of our programmes.

---

36   2   Listen to a conversation between Harold Schumann and
François Trudeau, the Personnel Manager.

3   Read the following memo from François Trudeau to
Vera Jones.

Date: 30th June, 1983

To: Vera Jones   From: François Trudeau
      Training Manager (Courses)   Personnel Manager

Subject: Special Courses

I just want to let you know how sorry I am all this couldn't be much
easier.   The choice to me seems quite clear. Harold just hasn't
got your experience - besides I think the job'naturally'belongs to
you. I will certainly speak to Richard Maas on your behalf. In the
meantime I think it would be better if you didn't'campaign'on your
own behalf.

---

4   Richard Maas has prepared a confidential report for the
board on both Schumann and Jones.

Read the following extract from his report on Schumann.

The majority of people who need to follow these training
programmes are men. On the sales and marketing side this is
exclusively the case. Harold Schumann has built up a great
rapport with the representatives in sales and marketing, and
indeed with the representatives in other departments. I think it
fair to say that he represents the training department in the best
possible light.

5 With the information you have gained so far make recommendations in a short report which will go to the board for their consideration. You should also consider the following information:

	Vera Jones	Harold Schumann
Age	43	36
Salary	$35,000	$41,000
Previous experience	Secretary in Personnel Dept. Personnel Officer	Salesman and Sales Trainer with another company
Languages	English	French, German, English
Length of time with company	10 years	4 years

  6 It is nine months later. Listen to the tape. You will hear Jan de Wit, the Assistant Training Manager, speaking to the newly appointed Training Manager.

7 What should be the course of action when a service, such as in-company training, starts to attract fewer participants?

8 Read the following memo from Richard Maas, sent to the Training Manager.

<u>Date</u>: 21st March, 1984

  <u>To</u>: Harold Schumann   <u>From</u>: Richard Maas
       Training Manager   Managing Director

<u>Subject</u>: Training Courses

In the last six months I note that the response to our training courses has dropped by 25%. I further note that your department is well over budget — by 30%. This morning I received a disturbing phone call from the Sales Department about the quality of the present programme. Please meet me tomorrow at 10.00 a.m. to discuss this.

Discuss what action Maas should take. You should also consider the following:

     The Training Manager is required to give and be given six months notice.

     Vera Jones, has now secured employment elsewhere.

7 A QUESTION OF INNOVATION

LANGUAGE REVIEW: Stating requirements; Giving reasons

Stating requirements

Elite, a company which produces cosmetic products, recently launched a new range of fragrances with new bottle shapes. However, the special design feature of geometrically shaped bottles and caps has caused production problems in the printing stage. They are now looking for a replacement for their existing ink transfer machine, which will be able to print successfully onto these new bottles and caps.

Mary Rodgers of the Production Department is calling IMM, a company which produces a range of bottling and packaging machinery. She has been put through to Jim Reeves of the Sales Department.

 38 1 Listen to the conversation and answer the questions.

Telephoning a Why is Mary Rodgers ringing Jim Reeves?

b What is the specific problem with their printing machine?

c What shape are the bottle caps?

d What are the caps made of?

e What is the speed of the existing machine?

f Which machine does Jim Reeves suggest?

g Jim offers to send something to Mary. What is it?

2 Mary Rodgers describes some of the basic requirements for the new ink transfer printing machine. These are summarised below. Listen to the conversation again and pick out the phrase she uses to introduce these requirements. Follow the example.

	Requirement	Phrase
a	A replacement for one of our ink transfer printing machines.	*We're looking for . . .*
b	A machine which will give us more flexibility and allow us to print on just about any shape.	
c	Capable of printing on fragile materials.	
d	A procedure that's easy to set up, so that we can handle short runs of our different product lines.	
e	Multi-colour printing for some of our lines.	
f	A facility for both single and multi-colour printing.	

3 Read this letter Mary Rodgers wrote to another company, Spectrum, which also produces a range of ink transfer printing machines.

Dear Sirs,

We are a company which produces perfumes and cosmetics. Recently we introduced a new range of fragrances, and we find that our existing ink transfer machine is not coping with the new geometric shape of both our bottles and bottle caps. We are therefore seeking a replacement and believe your range of machines could be of interest to us.

Our current requirement is for a machine which will enable us to print on a variety of surface shapes. As the majority of the bottles and caps we use are made of glass or plastic, it must be capable of printing on fragile surfaces. We also have to handle short rather than continuous runs in our bottling process, and therefore we require the machine to have an easy set-up procedure.

Finally, we occasionally have a need for multi-colour printing so obviously our preference will be for a machine which would give us this additional flexibility.

Could you please let us know if you have a machine which fits in with the requirements outlined above, and if so whether it would be possible for you to arrange a demonstration.

We look forward to hearing from you.

Yours faithfully,

a Pick out the expressions she uses to state her requirements.

b In what ways do these expressions differ from the spoken forms as used in the phone conversation?

The Purchasing Department of Elite is interested in finding an alternative supplier of bottles for their range of fragrances. The requirements are as follows:

material	glass for bottles plastic for caps
colours	clear for bottles white/yellow for caps
bottle sizes	10 ml/15 ml/20 ml/25 ml
basic shapes	cylindrical/oval/rectangular

4   As a member of the Purchasing Department of Elite contact the following two companies. State your requirements and request information.

a   Telephone the Sales Department of Carnation, a British company which produces various glass and plastic containers.

b   Write a letter to Vidrerias SA in Bilbao who also produce bottles for the fragrance industry.

Giving reasons

This checklist identifies some of the important areas which should be investigated before launching a new product.

1   Explain why any company which is involved in new product development needs to consider these points.

Checklist for launching new products

The identification of the potential customer.

The type of distribution system (wholesaler, direct to customer, exclusive distributor).

The type of advertising message.

The ability of the current sales organisation to handle the project.

The competitors and their reputation.

The likely effect of the new product on existing production.

Government measures which could affect production or sales.

The exact cost of the different stages of product development, design, packaging, advertising and promotion.

The effect of the new product on any existing lines.

The timing of the new product launch.

The extra costs for materials, tools, personnel.

The expected profit margin.

2   The extract below from a book on marketing gives five reasons for using market research.

a   As you read the extract pick out the word or expression which signals each reason.

b   Then complete the notes on the right. The first part has been done for you.

Market Research	*Reasons*	*Signal*
There are many reasons behind the increasing use of market research techniques, both for consumer and industrial products.		
Firstly, marketing departments need market research in order to monitor technological change not only within their own industry but also in the industries which use the product.	to monitor technological change	in order to
Secondly, it is needed for more accurate information about trends and changes in market demand.		
Another important reason for using market research is to obtain more complete information on competitors. In this way management can react more quickly to changes in competitors' products and policies. The marketing department also needs to be able to assess potential in a variety of areas including product development so that it can reduce risk, and here too market research can help.		
Finally, some companies are rarely aware of what is happening in their own markets because there is no direct contact between producers and end users. Market research can be used to bridge the information gap between producer and customer.		

3   Match the information in the right and left columns, and link the two ideas using **so that, to, in order to, for.**

Requirements	*Reasons*
a Research must be limited during the early stages of development.	The product can be constantly modified to fit the consumer's requirements.
b Managers directing new products need to have backing from top management.	More complete information about customer's needs.
c You've got to use the most up-to-date market research techniques.	Keep up the timetable momentum and keep down up-front investment.
d It's necessary to get regular feedback from potential customers.	Prevent resources from being diverted to support existing products.

Describing procedures

The following text describes the sequences or steps which must be carried out before a new medical product becomes available to doctors and patients.

1   Read the extract and answer the questions in the margins.

There are seven stages. **First of all** a new substance is tested under laboratory conditions to establish its pharmacological effectiveness, and to determine its possible side effects and toxicity. If the tests are successful, the substance is **then** tested on volunteers to check if there are any adverse effects which have not shown up in the laboratory. If no such effects appear a clinical trials licence is **then** applied for from the government authorities concerned, so that the product can be evaluated by hospital specialists, following carefully specified procedures. **The fourth and fifth stages** involve the analysis of information from the previous clinical trials and the publication of results through the medical press. **Following this** the accumulated data is presented to the Committee on the Safety of Medicine, who rule on the drug's suitability for general use. Only **then, after** the granting of the licence, can the final step be taken – the introduction and marketing of the product.

a   List the 7 stages.

b   Identify the function of the words in **bold type.**

c   Which verbs are used to describe the sequence? What do you notice about these verbs?

39   *Fiona Thompson works in the research laboratory of Smart and Craven, a major pharmaceutical company.*

2   Listen to her describing the same procedure and then answer the questions below.

a   What differences do you notice between the style of the written text and the spoken description?

b   The following words, phrases and sentences are taken from the written extract above. Find the phrases used by Fiona Thompson in her talk which are equivalent in meaning to the phrases below:

... to establish its pharmacological effectiveness

... to determine its possible side effects and toxicity

If the tests are successful

If no such effects appear

The fourth and fifth stages involve

... the accumulated data is presented

... the Committee on the Safety of Medicine, who rule on the drug's suitability

Only then, after the granting of the licence can the final step be taken

Notice the use of the present tense and the passive when describing sequences and procedures.

3   Discuss the chart below and decide what type of product it could apply to. Describe the sequence, and include expressions which make the order of steps clear.

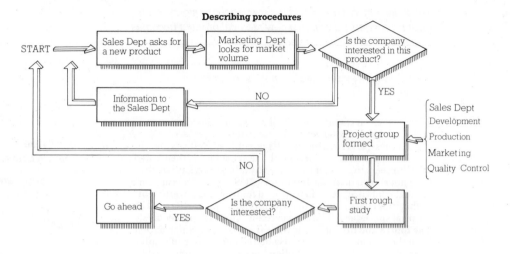

Describing procedures

4   The notes below describe stages in setting up a new computer project. Write a short summary of these stages including the objectives.

Stages	Objectives
Initial study of the problem	to assess the feasibility of solving the problem by computer to work out likely costs
Detailed study	to establish all the requirements of the system
Preliminary design	to evaluate alternative solutions to evolve optimum approach
Detailed design of selected system and preparation of computer programme specification	
Programme development – includes design of programme, preparation of supporting clerical procedures, management and user staff training and file creation	
Implementation – testing of entire system in a working environment	to detect potential problems
Operation – system in full use	

FOCUS ON INTERACTION

David Rowlinson is the Head of the European Research and Development Department of IT, an American oil company. The research department is based in England. One of the products they are developing, a new turbine oil, is undergoing field trials in Holland. Tom de Wey, the head of the Marketing Department there, is phoning David Rowlinson to discuss some problems they are having with this new product.

40 **1**   Listen to the end of the conversation, and answer the questions below.

Telephoning   **a**   Does David Rowlinson think the problem with the new turbine oil is very serious?

b   What does David suggest that Tom does?

c   Why can't David get the report back to Tom very quickly?

d   When is the annual planning meeting?
When does David Rowlinson think it is?

e   Where is the meeting going to take place?

f   How did David Rowlinson get the wrong date for the meeting?

2   Their conversation contained several examples of verbs + prepositions that are often used in everyday speech. Listen to the conversation again and complete the phrases below.

Send us . . . a sample

Any chance of getting a report . . . to me by Thursday?

I've got it (the meeting) . . . for the following week.

I noted it (the meeting) . . . myself.

I must have got the dates muddled . . .

3 Look at the two relevant extracts from Rowlinson's diary. What appointments will have to be cancelled? What alternative arrangements are possible for the following week?

Notes	Mr Imberti, Head of Production in Rome. Wed - Fri v! imp. Plan visit round Dept for Thurs p.m.	Meeting Brussels. Book flight for Thurs lunchtime	Notes
Monday 18		9.30 - 11.00 Progress Meeting 3.00 - 5.00 Interviews	Monday 25
Tuesday 19	Meeting Tom Gray 10.00 a.m.	B'ham Plant and heavy machinery exhibition	Tuesday 26
Wednesday 20	Mr Imberti arrives Meeting 2.00 p.m. Dinner 7.30 Grand Hotel	lunch with Mr McTavish 1.00 - 3.00 (White Horse)	Wednesday 27
Thursday 21	Tour of Dept with Mr Imberti 2.00 - 4.30 Meeting with Mr Jordan re BL hydraulic fluid	lunch time leave for Brussels	Thursday 28
Friday 22	Interview for trainee Ms Doyle 9.30 Farewell lunch Mr Imberti 1.00 p.m. White Horse	Meeting Brussels Planning group 9.00 a.m.	Friday 29
Saturday 23	Sunday 24	Sunday 31	Saturday 30

4 Listen to the telephone conversation between Rowlinson and Martha Ellis, Mr Jordan's secretary. Answer the questions below.

a Rowlinson wants to change the meeting. What expression does he use to introduce his request?

'I . . . change the date of the meeting.'

These are other expressions which could be used to introduce his request. Do they create exactly the same effect?

Please could we change the date of the meeting?

Would it be possible to change the date of the meeting?

I would like to change the date of the meeting.

b Martha Ellis tries to find out the most convenient day. What does she say?

'Which day . . . ?'

Can you think of any other expressions she could have used?

c How does Rowlinson reply?

'. . . the early part of the week.'

d Martha Ellis suggests Monday. What expression does she use?

'. . . Monday?'

What other phrases would be appropriate?

e She also suggests a time. What expression does she use?

'. . . we . . . 11.30?'

What other phrases would be appropriate?

5   Make any further phone calls necessary to re-arrange the diary for the end of the week. Try to get colleagues in the R and D department to take your place while you're in Brussels.

IT (Europe) is holding its annual planning meeting at the European headquarters in Brussels.

The meeting has two objectives:

to establish a list of priorities for development policy

to choose new research projects for the coming year

Their final decision must reflect both technical and marketing considerations.

Present at the meeting are:

James Finnigan	*President of IT (Europe)*
Phillipe Blanche	*Marketing Director (Europe)*
Arne Bergstrom	*Financial Director (Europe)*
David Rowlinson	*Head of R and D (Europe)*
Tom de Wey	*Head of Marketing (Holland)*

The five members of the planning committee are discussing one of the R and D proposals, to develop new hydraulic fluid for use in the motor industry.

Meetings

42

6   Listen to the extract from the meeting and answer these questions.

General questions

a   What reasons are given for and against the development of highly sophisticated hydraulic fluids for the motor industry?

b   How long will it take to develop this new product and why?

c   What is the general reaction to the length of the development period?

Language questions

a   James Finnigan starts the meeting. What does he say? Is this formal or informal?
What other expressions would be appropriate here?

b   James Finnigan asks Phillipe Blanche to speak first. What exactly does he say?

c   How does Phillipe Blanche emphasise that he believes the motor industry is important for IT?

d   Tom de Wey supports Phillipe Blanche and gives a further reason for concentrating on the motor industry. How does he introduce this reason?

e   Arne Bergstrom has certain reservations. He uses several rather negative phrases to introduce his doubts. What are they?

f Phillipe Blanche is unhappy about the development time. What expression does he use to make this quite clear? Is this expression strong, neutral or weak? What other expressions would create the same effect?

g David Rowlinson agrees with Tom de Wey that many of the tests and precautions in product development are too strict. What expression does he use?

Which of these have the same force?

That may be true
I see what you mean
I agree totally
Of course you're right

7 The phrases on the left were also used during the meeting. Match them with the correct description on the right. The first one has been done for you.

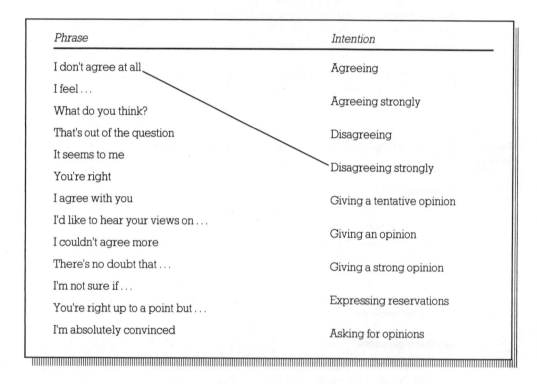

Phrase	Intention
I don't agree at all	Agreeing
I feel ...	
What do you think?	Agreeing strongly
That's out of the question	Disagreeing
It seems to me	
You're right	Disagreeing strongly
I agree with you	Giving a tentative opinion
I'd like to hear your views on ...	
I couldn't agree more	Giving an opinion
There's no doubt that ...	Giving a strong opinion
I'm not sure if ...	
You're right up to a point but ...	Expressing reservations
I'm absolutely convinced	Asking for opinions

8 Animals are used both in the testing of industrial products such as hydraulic fluids and lubricants, and for pharmaceutical and cosmetic products. Prepare a case either to support or oppose this type of research.

Remember you are practising:
giving opinions
agreeing/disagreeing
persuading people to accept your point of view

ACTIVITIES

1   This diagram shows the interaction between the Marketing Department and the Development Laboratory in the development of a cosmetic product.

After discussion, make a short presentation. Describe the information flow, and explain what information is needed to develop a new product idea and why.

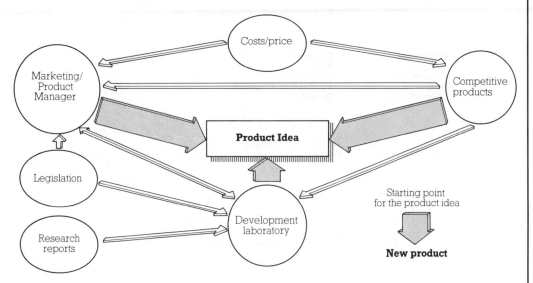

2   Draw a flow chart that shows the development stages of a product or system with which you are familiar. Then give a full presentation of this chart.

3   Many new-product attempts fail. A recent survey into reasons for new product failure highlighted the four points below, among other factors.

Lack of commitment from top management – plenty of initial support but too many technically feasible and marketable projects are abandoned halfway.

Bad new-product organisation. New-product responsibility is frequently given to managers who are already responsible for existing products. The result is that very often new-product development is given secondary importance to taking care of existing products.

The wrong managers are chosen to head new-product groups. Most frequently responsibility is given to managers of existing products and often such a manager does not have the necessary creativity, flair and willingness to take risks.

Concepts are over-researched and tested and this makes the process too expensive and too lengthy.

a   Do you think these are the most important reasons for new-product failure? Can you give examples from your own experience?

b   What other factors are involved in new-product failure?

4   Present a case history of product failure that you know about. Try to analyse the reasons why it failed.

The diagram below shows the sequence of stages from the receipt of a special tailor-made order to its eventual despatch to the customer.

5   Complete the diagram with the information below. Each of the pieces of information represents one stage in the procedure:

Production	**Customer**
Invoicing	**Pricing**
Acknowledgement	**Purchasing**
Despatch	**Production Planning**
Order in	**Design**

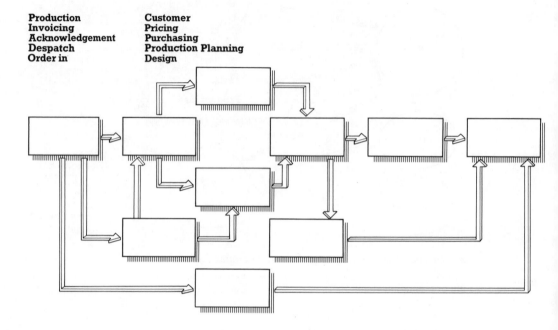

8 A QUESTION OF FACTS AND FIGURES

LANGUAGE REVIEW: Introducing consequences; Organising information

Introducing consequences

1   Below you will find some information about recent changes in the British car industry.

What are the probable implications for:

a   car production in Britain?

b   suppliers to the main car manufacturers?

c   the workforce?

> Car prices in Britain are up to 30% higher than in many other countries.
>
> In 1974 British car makers' output was 2m units a year. In 1980 output of the four main producers: Ford (American owned), British Leyland (State owned), Vauxhall (part of General Motors), Talbot (French owned) was about 900,000 units a year.
>
> Ford made about 4000 fewer cars in Britain in 1980 than in 1974 but has increased its share of the British market by importing fully built vehicles from its factories in West Germany, Belgium and Spain.
>
> Despite increases in productivity in the car industry, and the closure of some very old fashioned plants, productivity in some British plants is still below that in some Belgium and German plants.
>
> British Leyland, despite recent heavy cutbacks and the closure of plants is still dependent on government money to survive. It employs 130,000 people directly, and 130,000 indirectly in supplier companies. It also gives British Steel a quarter of its contracts.

2   Listen to the extract from a TV report on the future of the British car industry. What are the speaker's conclusions, and the *linking words* that introduce them? The first has been done as an example.

	Facts/Evidence	Linking words	Speaker's conclusion
a	Productivity and standards of workmanship are far lower than in the rest of Europe.	This means that ...	companies such as Ford would like to build cars outside Britain, e.g. in Belgium, Germany and Spain.
b	Ford is considering moving production from Britain to Belgium, Germany and Spain.		
c	Talbot's French owners are worried about the heavy losses in France and are facing pressure to invest in France rather than in Great Britain.		
d	BL employs 130,000 directly and 130,000 indirectly as suppliers. Contracts with BL represent a quarter of British Steel's work. Unemployment is rising.		

3   What are the implications and likely consequences of the following facts about the world economy? Use the prompts to introduce likely consequences.

a   High inflation rates have been reduced in many western countries.   (This means)

b   The price of oil tends to fluctuate.   (It follows therefore that)

c   The cost of borrowing money is still too high.   (So, it follows)

d   The Japanese are able to produce electronic goods at a much lower price than their European counterparts.   (Therefore)

e   Unemployment has been rising and competition for the remaining jobs is getting tougher.   (This is going to mean)

f   In the present economic climate many manufacturers prefer to buy cheaper steel from developing countries rather than steel produced in the West.   (The implication of this is that)

Organising information

1 Read the questions below and then look at the chart and report that follow.

a Identify the function of the words and phrases in **bold type.**

b Answer the questions in the margin on the right.

c Match each paragraph with the appropriate label choosing from the list opposite:

Conclusion
Third implication
First implication
Summary of the main facts
Second implication.
e.g. Paragraph 1 is the Introduction.

Changing demand for products (Europe)

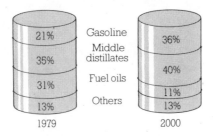

	Gasoline	
21%	Middle distillates	36%
35%		
31%	Fuel oils	40%
		11%
13%	Others	13%
1979		2000

This chart shows the expected changes in demand for oil products by the year 2000.

In 1979 British Petroleum estimated that some 35% of oil demand was for products **such as** industrial heating oil; another 31% for heavier fuel oils, **while** that for higher grade products, e.g. transport fuels, was only 21%. For the year 2000 **however**, the forecast is quite different. Heavy fuel oils are expected to account for only 11% as compared to 31%. Requirements for middle distillates should stay more or less the same, while demand for gasoline will increase to 36%.

> What does *that* refer to?

This new pattern of oil demand, with its emphasis on lighter products, and the declining demand for heavy products must have wide implications for the oil industry.

> What does *its* refer to?

Firstly, it means that refineries will have to be updated to concentrate on producing petroleum and other light products. So it follows that oil companies will have to press ahead with large scale investment in both building new refineries and installing greater conversion capacity for upgrading heavier products in the existing refineries.

> What does *it* refer to?

A second major implication of this new pattern of demand in the year 2000, which must be seen in the light of an overall decline in sales, is that many out-of-date refineries, especially those with the crudest type of refining processes, will have to be shut down completely.

> What does *those* refer to?

Finally, if we accept that the industry as a whole must invest in upgrading machinery to convert the unwanted heavy products, it could mean that lighter products will lose their scarcity value, and that would be bad news for the refining industry.

> What does *it* refer to?

---

2 Look at the charts on the right and discuss the implications for:

the environment

investment patterns for the oil companies

the economy of your own country

3 Write a short paragraph presenting your findings. Use the organisation of ideas in the report on Changing Oil Demands as a model.

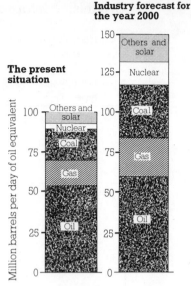

Industry forecast for the year 2000

The present situation

Million barrels per day of oil equivalent

LANGUAGE STUDY: Analysing influences; Criticising decisions

Analysing influences

1 Look at the graph on the right:

a What are the main discrepancies between the industry forecasts for the year 2000 and the public forecasts?

b Discuss any factors which you think may have influenced the way the public sees the future energy balance and divide these into definite and possible influences.

44 [cassette] **2** Listen to this extract from an interview with a representative of a major oil company.

a What does the speaker say about the future uses of:

solar power?

nuclear power?

oil?

b Both the speaker and the interviewer attempt to draw certain conclusions during the discussion.
Listen again and complete the following extracts from the discussion. Say whether the conclusions are **certain** or **tentative.**

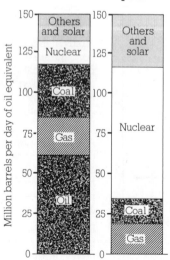

The year 2000

Industry forecast / **What the public expects**

Million barrels per day of oil equivalent

I '... this ... because there is a deliberate policy on the part of the energy companies to hide the facts from the public?

M No, it wouldn't be fair to say that. OK, the companies are trying to play down the future importance of nuclear power, and this ... related to the fact that nuclear power isn't popular with the public. But at the same time you've got to remember that the energy situation is constantly changing and soon becomes out of date. And this I think ... one of the main reasons why even the energy companies don't have a clear picture of the year 2000.'

3 Write a short paragraph analysing any of the factors which may explain the following trends.

a The difficulties of American car manufacturers.

b The increase in the number of small company bankruptcies.

c The collapse of many textile companies in Western Europe.

Criticising decisions

A new scheme of loans for small businesses has been set up for companies with a turnover of under £1m. David Cookson has applied to Central and City Bank for one of these loans. His plan is to set up a small factory which will produce garden furniture.

After Cookson's meeting with Derek Morgan at the bank the following note has been left for the Head of the Loans Department.

RE: APPLICATION FROM DAVID COOKSON
Don't think it's on. Recommend we turn down the application. I've some big doubts about: 1. Previous business record. Last two ventures failed.
    2. His honesty and frankness!
    3. Insufficient financial experience.

1 Listen to the conversation between Derek Morgan and his head of department and complete these sentences which identify some of the points he is worried about.

If he ... a better track record, I ... more confidence.

He ... tried to hide the facts.

They ... tried to get someone involved in the project.

If they ... a better management record, I ... it more consideration.

Robinsons', a small manufacturing company, are on the point of bankruptcy. A consultant has been called in to analyse and identify why this has happened. His main criticisms of their past policy are listed below, together with some of the consequences for the company.

2   Complete the list of consequences, and discuss what would have happened if the company had handled things differently.

Criticisms		Consequences
Many outstanding creditors	⟶	Poor cash flow and no work capital
Overstaffed	⟶	Large wage bill
Level of stock was too high	⟶	Cutback on production
Low advertising budget	⟶	Problems in reaching sales target
Little discussion of new ideas	⟶	Products rather out of date
Too few sales outlets	⟶	
No investment in new machinery for many years	⟶	
No long range planning	⟶	

FOCUS ON INTERACTION

John Fairfax is the owner of two small cruise ships and a fleet of charter yachts which operate in the Aegean.

His company, Sunshine Cruises, which was set up 8 years ago, exploited a gap in the cruise market for short duration luxury cruises which would appeal to business people in a high income bracket, but with limited time for holidays. Passengers are flown from London and New York to Athens where they join a ship for 7–9 days.

This venture was partly financed by a loan of £5m from one of the major banks, Central and City. The security against the loan was a mortgage on two cruise vessels worth £2m each, together with a number of smaller yachts and harbour offices valued at £3m. The cruises proved very popular and the venture was a considerable success.

Now, with a turnover of £10m, John Fairfax wishes to expand his fleet with two additional cruise ships. These would operate in the growing Caribbean market. Central and City have again been approached for an extension of the loan by £2m. The bank, however, is not happy about John Fairfax's expansion plans, and will only lend the additional money against increased security. Although John Fairfax has valuable assets in London – the lease on his central London offices, worth £250,000 and 2000 acres of agricultural land valued at £2000 an acre – he feels that the strength of his business should be sufficient security to cover the extension of the loan, and he is therefore unwilling to mortgage the lease on his London property.

46   *John Fairfax is at a party. Listen to the first part of the conversation where he is talking to his hostess, Sue Middleton.*

Socialising 1   Answer the following questions.

General Questions

a   Who is Mary and why isn't she at the party?

b   Who is David Greenaway?

c   How long is he going to be in London?

Language Questions

a   Do you think Sue and John Fairfax know each other:
     very well, well, slightly?
     What gives this impression?

b   Sue enquires about John's business. What exactly does she say?
     'How . . . ?'

c   John apologises because his wife is not with him.

     How does he introduce the apology?
     '. . . she couldn't come.'

d   Sue offers John Fairfax a drink. What does she say?
     Which of the expressions from the list below would also be appropriate in this context:
     Do you want a drink?
     Come over and get a drink.
     What about a drink?

e   Before Sue introduces John Fairfax to David Greenaway she gives John some basic facts about him.
     Why is she offering this information at this stage?

f   John Fairfax wants to know which company David Greenaway works for. What question does he ask?

2   Now listen to the second part of the conversation and answer the following questions.

General Questions

a   Where was David Greenaway before he moved to London?

b   Why does he suggest that John Fairfax telephone him the following week?

c   Why does John Fairfax bring the conversation to an end?

Language Questions

a   How does Sue introduce John Fairfax to David Greenaway?

     What other expressions could be used here?

b The speakers keep the conversation moving by asking each other questions. What are they?

Note down other topics which could be introduced at this stage of the conversation. What question forms would you use?

c Is John's reply to the question: 'Are they proving difficult?', affirmative or negative?

Does he think the bank is being a bit difficult or very difficult?

What is the exact expression he uses?

d David Greenaway suggests that John Fairfax should telephone the following week.

How does he introduce his suggestion? Complete the dialogue:

DAVID ... call me next week and we'll talk it over.
JOHN That's ... you. I ... that.

e Both Sue and John Fairfax leave David Greenaway to speak to other people at the party.

How do they bring their conversation with David to an end without appearing abrupt and rude?

Complete the dialogue:

SUE ... someone ... and I want ... with him.
JOHN But, ... I've ... someone I know from the shipyard and I need ... with him.

3 In the previous conversation, there were several examples of polite social exchanges where a quick and appropriate response is very important.

Match phrases from column A and B below to make short two-line dialogues.

A	B
How are you?	Fine.
Can I get you something to eat?	No really. This one's on me.
How are things?	I'm afraid not.
Have you time for a quick drink?	It's been nice meeting you.
How do you do?	I'm very pleased to meet you.
Goodbye.	I think I'll have some of that.
David, this is John Fairfax.	Thanks, but not at the moment.
Why don't you try some of this?	Thank you. It looks very good.
What would you like to eat?	How do you do?
I'll get this.	Not too bad.

An employee from one of your overseas branches is on a business trip and will spend 2 or 3 days in your company.

4   Decide on some details about the visitor. One person should introduce this colleague to other people. Now act out the conversation.

Peter Bellamy, a co-director of John Fairfax's company, is on a business trip to Sweden and is making a routine call to find out what has been happening in London.

Telephoning
47

5   Listen to the telephone call and answer the questions.

a   Why is John glad Peter has called?

b   What does Peter think has happened about the loan?

c   What, in fact, has happened?

d   How does Peter react to John's news about Fairchild's?

e   What tactics does John plan to use to make sure he gets the loan?

f   Peter is worried about John's plan. He gives two reasons. What are they?

g   What arguments does John use to try to allay his fears?

6   Look at the list of characteristics.

a   From what you know about the two men which of the characteristics below would you choose to describe each of them?

cautious	shrewd
impulsive	aggressive
indecisive	indiscreet
reserved	diplomatic

Find phrases on the tape which you could use to support your view.

e.g.   *'we can't lose'*, indicates a rather careless, impulsive attitude on John's part.

          'don't you think that's rather risky', shows more caution on Peter's side.

b   What do you notice about John's style of speaking compared to Peter's?

Later that week John Fairfax had a meeting with Ron Pickford, Head of the Loans Department of Central and City Bank. The bank continued to insist on additional security against the loan of the extra £2m. However, despite the fact that John had not yet received any written confirmation of the loan from Fairchild's, he felt sufficiently confident to write the following letter to Central and City Bank.

Letters **7** Read the letter and identify the function of the
underlined words and phrases.

Dear Mr Pickford,

RE: EXTENSION LOAN

I have now had a chance to discuss the details of our recent
conversation with my other directors.
<u>As I told you</u> then, the general opinion here is that the terms for
the loan extension are far too stiff, particularly as we have had an
excellent loan record in the past.
<u>Fortunately</u> we have been able to make alternative arrangements on
more acceptable terms, and we will, <u>therefore</u>, not be proceeding
with our loan application to you.
<u>I feel most strongly that</u> your board could have been more flexible
on the matter. As we are expanding rapidly and all the signs are
that this new venture will be a great success we would have preferred
to have continued our long relationship with you. <u>Nevertheless</u>, I am
sure you understand our point of view.

Yours sincerely

Meetings **8** Listen to the extract from the board meeting at
48 Fairchild's Bank.

a What is the bank's future loans policy going to be?

b Why has this decision been taken?

c What are the short term and long term implications of
this change in policy for John Fairfax.

d Identify any mistakes which John Fairfax has made in
handling the application for the loan. What can he do
now? How should he have handled it?

ACTIVITIES

*In the last few years the record industry has had a number of
financial crises.*

49   **1** Listen to this extract from a radio talk on the current
crisis in the recording industry.

Then read the report on the situation at Sounds Live, a British
record company.

Use the information on the tape and in the report to:
explain the company's present difficulties.
identify any mistakes which have been made.
draw parallels with other industries where similar
mistakes have been made.

Fears that Sounds Live would be facing heavy losses by this
financial year were confirmed by the annual figures released this
week. The company, which traditionally has been involved in
recording and the manufacture and distribution of records, is
facing serious financial problems. Efforts to diversify have done
nothing to stem the downhill trend and have, in fact, only served
to make the situation worse. In 1981, in answer to general
setbacks experienced throughout the record business, the
company obtained a significant loan to set up a new factory in

South Shields which, it was hoped, would improve productivity and allow them to reduce their overall wage bill. In addition, as part of a general survival strategy, the decision was also taken to branch out into the entertainments business, and with this in mind a number of clubs and theatres were bought.

This change in policy necessitated further loans and the company, despite improving sales figures, has been crippled by the huge interest payments on the loan.

2　Read the following and analyse why the company eventually had to close down?

Whose Advice to Take

For five years Clothespeg, a company which produces an inexpensive range of women's clothes, had been in a very bad financial situation, like many other companies in this sector. The company had been hit by rising wages and competition from low cost imports from Hong Kong and Taiwan.

The Managing Director, Daniel Peters, recognised the seriousness of the situation. It seemed to him the only solution was to spend their way out of the recession and invest in more up-to-date production facilities, at the same time rationalising production and producing higher quality garments where the profit margin was higher. Daniel Peters approached his bank for a loan, but the bank was cautious, and insisted that they called in an independent consultant before any decisions were taken regarding the loan.

The consultant came up with the following two-stage policy.

Stage 1: The manufacturing side of the business should be phased out. Initially one of the two factories would be closed. Some of the manufacturing of the cheaper lines would be transferred overseas and at the same time new lines would be imported direct from Hong Kong.

Stage 2: A Hong Kong office should be established to buy cheaper clothes, and a joint venture manufacturing project for the remaining product lines should be set up in Tunisia. Manufacturing in the UK would be abandoned.

When Shaun McGill, the Production Manager, heard about the plans he called a meeting to state his oppositon. He pointed out the effect of the redundancies in an area of already high unemployment and the impact this would have on their local suppliers and sub-contractors.

Daniel Peters respected Shaun McGill's opinion. He had been with Clothespeg since the beginning, 20 years ago. Perhaps he was right and anyway, did he really want to run a company involved only in importing and distributing?

After careful consideration Peters rejected the findings of the consultant. A new loan was organised with a different bank at a very high interest rate. The two factories were brought up to date with the loss of some jobs. At the same time Clothespeg bought out a number of companies with prestigious brand names. The idea was to give Clothespeg a new image. The company went from bad to worse and two months before was on the point of going into liquidation.

a　Was anyone responsible and would the result have been different if the consultant's advice had been followed?

b　Prepare a short report or presentation criticising company policy at Clothespeg. Your report should explain the situation and summarise the most important mistakes.

Case Study 2

Problems of distribution

Ashton is an American company which produces photographic equipment. Their range of slide projectors and screens is manufactured in Dallas, USA, and then distributed throughout the USA, and in ten different European countries. Their range of cameras is manufactured in Dallas, for the USA market, and also in Milan for the European market. Their European headquarters are in Marseille.

Over the past year various problems have arisen about the distribution of their products in Europe, the most serious of which has been delays caused by a lack of instruction leaflets to be inserted in each box. The company have therefore called in an independent consultancy group to pinpoint the cause and suggest some remedies.

50   1   Listen to this discussion between a consultant and one of Ashton's executives who is describing the basic distribution systems. As you listen complete the chart.

Chart 1

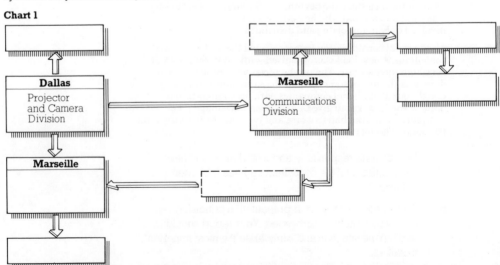

2   Now read this extract from the Ashton procedure document written two years ago on the subject of printing and insertion of instruction leaflets. Based on the information in the report complete the second chart below.

Re: Translation and Printing of Instruction Leaflets.

It has been decided that all leaflets for the European market should be translated and printed in Europe. Original text for all products will be sent from Dallas to the Communications Division in Marseille. From there they will be sent out to individual European subsidiaries for translation, and then returned to the Communications Division for typesetting and preparation of all artwork. Final artwork with text will be checked by individual subsidiaries. The Communications Division will then produce the final film for printing, which will be done in Marseille. All camera leaflets will be sent to Milan for inclusion with cameras; leaflets for other products will be packed in appropriate boxes before despatch from Marseille.

Chart 2

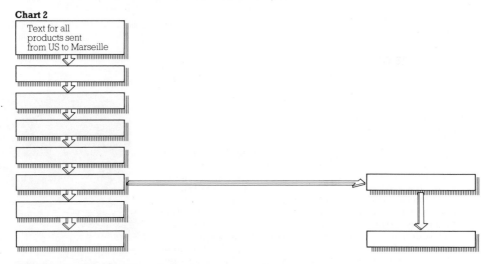

3   Having looked at how the basic systems work, try to identify the problem areas and the causes of these problems. Then compile a list of questions which you would like to put to those Ashton executives directly involved in the area of distribution. You should try to assess their attitude and opinions, get their suggestions for any change together with their reasons, and collect any financial evidence for or against their opinions. Background information is in the Teaching Guide.

The following Ashton executives should be interviewed at least once and re-interviewed if necessary:

Head of Communications Division, Marseille

Head of Personnel at European HQ, Marseille

Head of Corporate Communications, USA

Head of Camera Division, Milan

Head of Projectors Division, USA

Head of Ashton Subsidiary, Finland

4   Having interviewed the Ashton executives, pool all the information you have extracted and try to reach a conclusion. Then prepare and present a report and a presentation to the company giving your findings and recommendations.

9 A QUESTION OF SAFETY AND THE ENVIRONMENT

LANGUAGE REVIEW: Using negatives

||||||||||||||||||||||||||||||||||||||||||||||||||||||||||||||||||||||||||||||||||||||||||||||||||||||||||||||||||||||||||||||||||||||||||||||||||||||||||||||||||||||

Using negatives

1   The following extract describes the responsibilities of a clerical worker involved in dealing with orders and deliveries.

These days my job involves only a little typing. In fact **the title secretary is rather misleading.** However, my work does include the use of a terminal which is connected to the main computer in Stuttgart. When an order is received, I key the details in straightaway. These are transmitted to the factory. The following day the goods are despatched from the factory. **They by-pass us and are sent** direct to a central depot outside town, and from there to the dealer. **If we are unable to service the order immediately, the factory informs me,** and I in turn inform the dealer. **My responsibility ends here as it is the dealer who informs the customer.** A copy of all transactions is kept. This includes print-outs of everything sent out by us, and everything that is sent to us. My main concern is to make sure I have records of everything and that I know exactly where the information is. This means having a system **which always works well.**

a   Draw a diagram which shows the flow of information and goods.

b   Find other ways of expressing the phrases in **bold type.**

51   2   Listen to the same clerical worker talking about responsibilities. Pick out the expressions she uses in this spoken version which correspond to the phrases in **bold type** in the written version.

3   Listen to another speaker talking about his job routines.

a   Say if the following are true or false about the first speaker.

The speaker is a farmer.

The speaker is worried about money.

The speaker says it is possible to avoid damage.

b What type of job you think he has?

c What is his 'attitude' towards the environment?

d The following statements refer to ideas expressed on the tape. How does the speaker express these ideas?

Minimum damage means lower compensation.

It's very difficult to avoid some damage.

It's against our interests to set up expensive procedures.

e What effect does the speaker achieve by using negatives?

4 Read the following extract from a conversation between two people who work for an international construction company. Pick out the negative forms they use when arguing with each other.

A This project mustn't overrun. We've got to finish it by the end of May.

B But it's impossible. We can't do it by then.

A Look, if we don't get it done we'll incur penalty payments.

B Then why weren't we more realistic about the completion date in the original bid?

Now continue the conversation in a similar style, using the prompts below.

A That completion date necessary – otherwise no contract

B Not able complete job unless employ more workers

A Impossible – too expensive – project already over budget

B Not complete project on time – penalty payments

5 The two reports below are about accidents at work. After reading them explain what happened, emphasising the potential danger and need for precautions. Use negatives.

a The operation of these machines produces a small amount of dust. Without regular cleaning the dust starts to build up. It then becomes a safety hazard, as it catches fire very quickly and very easily. Any open flame, or spark, must be avoided. Our findings indicate that in this case the operator of the machine joined the company only three weeks ago. He was obviously unaware of the importance of the no-smoking sign. His burns, for the most part, are on the upper part of his body, mainly his arms and face.

b The woman in question was walking across the floor behind the assembly line. During the washing process two pipes, one for hot and another for cold water, are brought across from the water outlet on the wall. There is also a pipe to remove the dirty water. The washing process occurs only once every four hours, and then only for 10 minutes. For this reason the general warning about obstructions was overlooked. As already stated, the woman was carrying a heavy crate. She was unfamiliar with procedures at the assembly line and was therefore unprepared for the pipes across the floor.

Presenting information

52   1   Listen to the following presentation and read the script as you listen. Then answer the questions in the margin.

Our immediate concern should be with the Garrick Residential Zone. THIS AREA, which now contains more than 300 houses, a small shopping centre and a school, was once part of a large parcel of land of which we owned about a quarter. THIS PIECE of land was on high ground. The company first bought the land back in the 1920s, and intended in those days that it would eventually be built on. **However**, after the expansion of the main factory and the increase in the volume of waste products, we decided to use the land as a tip for waste. **Accordingly**, in the 1950s three large holes were dug, and waste material from the factory was buried in them. THIS was done with the permission of the authorities. *At no time did we act without following all established safety procedures.*

In the early 1960s the holes were filled in. THIS was because some of the traditional waste products from the main factory were now capable of being treated and recycled. OTHER PRODUCTS had to be disposed of with greater care. When we were approached to sell our piece of the land in 1964 the time was right. We had no real need for it.

Also, the owners of the land next to ours were very eager to sell. In 1965 the sale went through. Garrick obtained permission to build and by 1970 he had started. As it happened the part of the zone which used to belong to us became the site of the school, and of about fifty of the houses.

Two years ago, tests carried out on the drinking water in the area disturbed the health authorities. They came back to us and suggested that there was a connection between the contaminated water and our waste. We were able to disprove THAT quite easily. Water on the Garrick Residential Zone is pumped in from five miles away. **However**, several children started to fall ill. They developed skin irritations and other symptoms. In the last few months the health authorities have returned to the residential zone, and this time they have found two very small streams of water, badly contaminated with chemicals. Our sites were situated on high ground. The streams of water only appear after heavy rain. The suggestion is that chemicals from our old waste tips are being washed slowly through the ground, and that they actually come to the surface, as in these two small streams.

Naturally, I'm concerned. We must give this matter our full attention.

What is the purpose of the statements in *italics*? How do they relate to the rest of the presentation?

What is the purpose of the words in **bold type**?

What do the words in CAPITALS refer back to?

2   Who do you think is making this presentation, and who you think the audience is?

3 Go back through the presentation and list the different tenses used to describe the events which have led to the current problem.

4 Seven key dates mentioned in the presentation are listed below. What actions are associated with these dates? Complete the chart, following the examples.

Time	Active action	Passive action
In the 1920s	The company bought the land back	
In the 1950s		3 holes were dug
In the early 1960s		
In 1964		
In 1965		
In 1970		
Two years ago		

5 Draw a time chart, showing a similar sequence based on your own experience, e.g. product development, career development, company decline or growth, etc. This should include six separate dates. Then give a short presentation.

53 **6a** Listen to the following extracts from three separate interviews. Notice how the interviewer confirms and checks his facts, and how the speaker justifies what has been done.

b Now build up similar interviews around the following topics:

more rigorous safety regulations in the construction industry

the decision to withdraw a drug from the market

stricter regulations concerning computer security

the intervention by health inspectors in a fruit canning company

the introduction of a clocking-in system

Speaker A should check and confirm the facts.

Speaker B should justify the action, beginning each reply with one of the following phrases:

this was done

this was/is because

this/that had to be done

Questioning

The following telephone conversation between a local politician and a resident again concerns the pollution in the Garrick Residential Zone, which seems to be affecting the local school.

1   Read the dialogue and pick out any examples of negative questions.

LOCAL POLITICIAN
Yes, I fully understand your concern, Mrs Jones.

MRS JONES
But don't you think something should be done about it?

LOCAL POLITICIAN
I promise you that we're all very worried about the situation, Mrs Jones. The matter has been raised between the school and the local education authorities, and the local health authorities.

MRS JONES
Then why haven't you done anything? My daughter's ill. My friend's children are ill. Isn't that enough?

LOCAL POLITICIAN
Mrs Jones, I know about your daughter. I know about all the children.

MRS JONES
Shouldn't the school be closed? Everybody knows the children are being poisoned. It's not safe.

LOCAL POLITICIAN
Mrs Jones, the children are not being poisoned, and we don't know yet if the school is unsafe. The proper tests haven't been carried out yet.

MRS JONES
And how long will that take? A month? A year? I know what you people are like. Why can't we get a clear answer?

LOCAL POLITICIAN
The problem is that in situations like this people can jump to the wrong conclusions, Mrs Jones. We don't yet know all the facts, and it may turn out that the problem, if indeed there is a real problem, will be easy to solve. We need time.

MRS JONES
But isn't it true that you've already got the information?

54   2   Now listen to the tape and decide if these questions are being used to:

    suggest an action

    check information

    criticise

Note: In the conversation, Mrs Jones was using negative questions. These are forceful and are often used in arguing a case (see Unit 3).

3 A newly appointed Computer Manager in a medium sized company has recently set up new security procedures in his department, limiting access to authorised personnel only.

The extracts below come from a recent conversation which took place in the computer department.

a One of the two speakers is the Computer Manager. Who do you think the other speaker is?

b What do you think has happened?

c Place each extract under the correct heading.

Criticising
Checking
Suggesting

Extracts

Shouldn't we give some more thought to finding a procedure which will really work?

Didn't he check with you before he came in?

Wouldn't it be a good idea to hold some kind of meeting to inform people why we've tightened up security?

Isn't he from our Sales Department?

Hasn't everyone been informed about the new regulations?

Wasn't he in here a few days ago?

Don't you keep a watch on who's coming and going in the department?

Isn't the whole area meant to be properly secured?

Couldn't we restrict the closed-off area to the central computer area only?

Don't you see how important security is?

Don't you see that people are still getting in here without getting clearance first?

Don't you think the system's rather extreme?

Doesn't everybody realise that to come in here you've got to have a pass?

Wouldn't it be true to say that no one's taking these new regulations very seriously?

d Build up the dialogue that took place between the two speakers, and act it out.

Don't you think you should carry out more random checks, Mr Jones?

FOCUS ON INTERACTION

DGM AG is an Austrian company specialising in power stations. Over the last 50 years it has built many power stations in Europe and overseas, especially in South America. The company is now involved in pulling down a South American station it built 30 years ago, and rebuilding it to more modern specifications. The new project is a joint venture with an American consortium. Manuel Stillman works as a consultant for the Ministry of Industry, and coordinates much of the work done between DGM and the host country. He is writing to Johann Meyer, the Managing Director of DGM.

> Dear Mr Meyer,
>
> I am very concerned about recent developments here on the site. I am particularly concerned about recent reports in the local press. It appears that there is a large amount of asbestos in the old power station, especially around the boilers and pipes. This is now being disturbed by the workers as they take the old plant down. I do not need to stress the dangers in this. The local press has taken up the story and is showing a great deal of interest.
>
> In brief they claim that your American partners, Drew Engineering, are employing unskilled labour on the site, and providing them with little or no protection. This is quite contrary to agreements between your company and our government.
>
> I must stress that the situation is very serious. The work of dismantling the old asbestos lining should have been carried out by an experienced team. The fact that it has not endangers not only the workers themselves but the inhabitants of the surrounding area.
>
> I look to you, as Managing Director of the senior company in this joint venture, to sort this matter out immediately. I am requesting a meeting between you and Robert Stephens of Drew Engineering, London, next March 14th to discuss the matter further.
>
> Yours sincerely

The second letter is from Meyer to Stephens at Drew Engineering.

> Dear Bob,
>
> Further to my call today I'm enclosing the letter written recently by Manuel Stillman. As I pointed out he suggests March 14th, which is nearly six weeks away. In spite of the tone of the letter he doesn't seem to be in that much of a hurry.
>
> However, could you ring me next week when you've had time to think things over? I'd like your suggestions about what tactics we should use, and what we're going to do in the meantime.
>
> With regards.

Letters

1a The tone of the first letter is very strong. What phrases indicate this? Re-write the letter, showing greater familiarity between the two men, and less of a threatening overtone.

b Write a formal reply from Meyer to Stillman, saying that you will look into matters immediately. Discuss what other contents the letter should have.

c Act out the telephone conversation between Stephens and Meyer, when Stephens calls to discuss Stillman's complaint.

Johann Meyer has called an emergency meeting prior to the meeting with Manuel Stillman. Present at the meeting are:

Johann Meyer, (DGM); Robert Stephens, (Drew Engineering); Mary Greenwood, (Drew Engineering, Public Relations); Gunter Niemann, (DGM, Safety Officer).

Meetings
55 📼

2a Look at the script below of part of the meeting and complete it as you listen.

b Notice how the speakers stress the words in **bold type**. Why are they doing this?

MEYER … that there's been a serious mistake on our part. The point **now** is what we're going to do about it.

STEPHENS Mary has prepared a special report which we'll show you later on. … that it's going to help explain the situation and generally calm things down.

GREENWOOD That's right. … we've said that all activities will cease until the middle of March, as we are running ahead of other projects in the programme. We've explained that as we are very **concerned** about asbestos hazards this period of time will **also** give us the opportunity to introduce even **newer** and **more** up-to-date techniques.

NIEMANN That's right, but it seems we have had a serious breakdown between DGM and Drew. **Here** at DGM we thought **you** would be supervising all safety regulations. After all, it is **your** team that is demolishing the plant …

c Repeat the dialogue, trying to imitate the stress and intonation pattern.

In this further extract of the same meeting the group are thinking ahead to their meeting with Manuel Stillman.

3 Listen to the extract, and notice the following negative questions that are used.

Don't you think that we should try to convince Stillman that we have everything under control?

Couldn't you arrange that, Mr Niemann?

Isn't it your company who should provide this security?

Shouldn't we decide right now the lines of responsibility?

Wouldn't it be possible to publish our own report in the local press?

a Why have the speakers chosen to use negative questions?

b Ask the questions in a different way.

c   Find four suggestions that are made in the course of the meeting. How are they made?

d   When Meyer says: 'It should have been clearly stated in the first place', what is he really saying?

e   Rephrase the following, so that it has the same strength: 'The last thing we want is open discussion.'

ACTIVITIES

The Kelling Group

Kelling AB	Gothenburg (HQ)
Kelling (UK) plc	Birmingham
Kelling SA, France	Toulouse
Kelling SpA, Italy	Turin
Kelling NV., Belgium	Antwerp
Kelling AG, Germany	Essen
Total workforce	62,000
Products	Boilers, Metal Tubes, Insulation Materials, Tools.
Company language	English

The Kelling group is a Swedish multinational which, among other products, produces boilers and furnaces, and insulation materials.

The company has been using a chemical for the past 18 months in its insulation products which was developed in its own laboratories in Gothenburg. This chemical has proved extremely satisfactory, in terms of cost and efficiency. It has given the product a real edge on the international market.

Recently, however, a lab assistant in the company's largest subsidiary, in England, conducted some tests of his own and came up with some disturbing results. He discovered that when the chemical is sprayed on to insulating boards, walls and other linings, a vapour is given off which he claims could encourage skin cancer.

The assistant reported his findings to his superiors and they have forwarded the results to Sweden. The Chief Executive of the Swedish company then authorised the Research Lab in Gothenburg to test the chemical on rats. Prior to the news from England the Research Lab had found nothing dangerous in the chemical.

1   Act out two meetings:

a   Between the marketing representatives from England, Sweden, France, Italy, Germany and Belgium.

b   An executive meeting between the Chief Executive, the International Marketing Director, the Head of Research, the Public Relations Manager Sweden, the Factory Manager France, the Factory Manager Italy.

Roles for both meetings are in the Teaching Guide.

10   A QUESTION OF INFORMATION

LANGUAGE REVIEW: Talking about procedure

Talking about procedure

1   The company memorandum below was distributed throughout the offices of Hendriks, a company in Belgium manufacturing agricultural machinery. The company language is English. Read it, and use the information in the memorandum to carry out the tasks below.

> Paul Van Doorn takes over this month as Parts and Spares Manager.
> He replaces Gordon Sinclair, who will be returning to England after
> nearly six years in the job. Paul Van Doorn comes to us from
> Rotterdam, where he was Parts and Spares Manager for Hendriks, Holland.
> Coinciding with his taking over the job there will be a new proce-
> dure which all sales representatives and dealers should follow. This
> is explained in detail on sheet 478 (sent separately 11/4/83).
> It means that, whereas in the old system all requests for spares
> had to go first through Accounts, they will now be sent by computer
> straight to the warehouse. Mr Van Doorn is eager to see a more
> efficient flow of information operating in the whole Parts and
> Spares Division, and feels that this move will speed the process
> up considerably.

a   Why do you think all requests had to go first through Accounts?

b   Decide on what you think the old system was. Draw a chart to show the flow of information. Show what happened if the spares were not available.

c   Draw a chart to show the new system. Again, show what happens if the spares are not available.

56 2a   Now listen to a conversation between Paul Van Doorn and his assistant, Roberto Vittoni. Listen first for general comprehension.

b   Vittoni is interrupted twice. In groups discuss what you think he was going to say.
    We always . . .
    Yes, I . . .

3 Listen to the tape again, and find the sentences which tell you that these statements are correct. The first has been done as an example.

		Extract from tape
a	It's impossible to understand why Mr Sinclair kept to the old system.	*What I can't understand is why Mr Sinclair kept to the old one (system).*
b	There is no need for requests to go first to Accounts.	
c	It is necessary, however, for Accounts to know of the order.	
d	It is very important to work efficiently.	
e	Reducing unimportant stages is essential.	
f	Van Doorn is confident that the new system will improve the procedure.	

4a First, look at the following expressions and decide on what they mean.

You must come	You've got to come
We must be there	You can't read this
It must be my wife	I can't come
You should come	It can't be ours
You should wait	You could attend the meeting
He should be back	I could get there
You will come	You needn't come
I will be at the meeting	We oughtn't to do it

57 **b** Now listen to the expressions as they occur in the statements on the tape. Perhaps you now have a different idea about what some of them mean. Say what the difference is.

Patrick Jameson is the Service Manager of the UK subsidiary of Hendriks. The UK company assembles some of the machines in their factory in Bedford, but all spare parts must be ordered from Belgium.

The telex below was sent by Patrick Jameson to Jules Grandier, the Warehouse Manager in Belgium.

```
ATTN  JULES GRANDIER
CAN YOU PLEASE LET ME KNOW WHEN WE CAN EXPECT DELIVERY OF
THE APRIL ORDER FOR SPARE PARTS.
ALSO CAN YOU PLEASE CONTACT ME TODAY WITH DETAILS AS TO WHEN
WE CAN EXPECT DELIVERY OF OUTSTANDING SPARES.   PURCHASE
ORDER NUMBER 3642/14/295.   THIS ORDER IS NOW 6 WEEKS OVERDUE
AND HAS BECOME VERY URGENT.
REGARDS  P. JAMESON
```

5   The notes below were given by Jules Grandier to his secretary as the basis for a memo to his assistant. Complete the memo that the secretary has written. Use the following verbs: must (3), can't, needn't, should

> RE TELEX FROM HENDRIKS UK
> Order 3642/14/295 despatched two weeks ago. Suspect problem en route. Customs? Check it out please.
> Absolutely necessary to trace order before Van Doorn finds out. He won't be very happy. Very important to ring Jameson back, but not really necessary until I get him delivery dates for completion of April order.

> Regarding telex from Hendriks I have the despatch details for order
> 3642/14/295. So they .... be held up at the warehouse.
> They .... be delayed en route, perhaps with Customs. We ....
> find out what is going on. The new Spares Manager Paul Van Doorn
> is very keen on efficiency. You .... get back to Mr Jameson as
> soon as possible, but you .... do it until I've got more
> information on the delivery date to complete the April order. That
> .... keep him happy until I sort out the missing order.

6   Act out the eventual telephone call, by Grandier's assistant to Jameson at Hendriks UK. Details of the roles are in the Teaching Guide.

7   Read the following dialogue, and answer the questions in the margin. Claire Brown, who used to deal with requests for spares after they had been through Accounts, is phoning Bruno Chirac, one of the sales representatives.

CHIRAC	What do you mean, it's not your job any longer?	
BROWN	Just that. I don't deal with spares now. I've been put in charge of invoicing.	What has happened?
CHIRAC	I don't understand. Why wasn't I told?	What is his complaint?
BROWN	Look, Bruno. You must have known about it. It's not my job to tell you. Everyone was informed.	What is Claire Brown sure that Bruno Chirac knows?
CHIRAC	Well, I wasn't. Now, what about my last order?	
BROWN	It should have gone to Grandier in the warehouse. He's dealing with it all now.	What didn't happen?
CHIRAC	But it was sent to you.	
BROWN	If that's the case, then I haven't got it. Anyway, you ought to have followed the new procedure.	What didn't he do?
CHIRAC	What new procedure?	
BROWN	Bruno? Are you sure the problem is at our end?	
CHIRAC	What are you getting at?	
BROWN	Look, I know that your assistant – what's his name – was sent all the details about the new procedure some time ago. Sheet 478, I think. Yes, I know he was told.	What happened?
CHIRAC	I see. Well, I'll look into it. And you say that Grandier is dealing with spares now?	
BROWN	Yes, you don't have to send the request to Accounts any longer. The system has been changed.	What isn't necessary? What has happened?
CHIRAC	Well, that may be. But it's the first I've heard of it.	

8   Bruno Chirac now questions Pierre Corot, his assistant, about the new procedure. What does he want to know, and what mood is he probably in?

Complete the following opening phrases.

a   Pierre, were you...?

b   Have you been...?

c   Did you know that the system...?

d   When you get information, you...

e   It's absolutely necessary...

f   I must....

g   You ought to...

h   You ought to have...

i   I should have...

j   That last request should...

9   Act out a short conversation between Chirac and Corot. Chirac's objective is to make sure that Corot never keeps information from him again. Corot tries to make excuses. He does not want to take the blame.

LANGUAGE STUDY: Information flow

Information flow

The diagram below shows the flow of information between departments of a company which sells a technical product. The company receives a request for a special design from one of its customers.

1   Discuss the flow of information. Say if you think any link has been left out. Do you feel the flow could be different, or should be different?

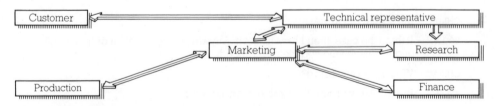

2   Discuss the kind of information you think will be moving in the directions indicated by each of the arrows.

Specify in more detail the information required at one or more of the stages in the diagram, e.g.

Research ◄—► Marketing
Marketing ◄—► Production
Finance ◄—► Marketing
Technical representative ◄—► customer

3   The diagram below shows different activities in a sequence where a car manufacturer attempts to improve his product by very careful analysis of his competitors' products.

a   Arrange the activities in the correct sequence.

b   Say at what stages there will be outward and inward flows of information. Say what type of information this will be.

Analyse the components

Analyse the market

Strip the car down

Specify changes to own product

Purchase competitors' cars

Analyse the competition

Discuss the findings

TDC (UK), a British subsidiary of an American company, assembles and sells computer terminals for the European market. The assembled terminals are sold both in the UK and in Europe.

4   The following diagrams show what happens:

inside the factory, after the assembly is complete. (Fig. 1)

when the terminals are sent to a customer in Europe. (Fig. 2)

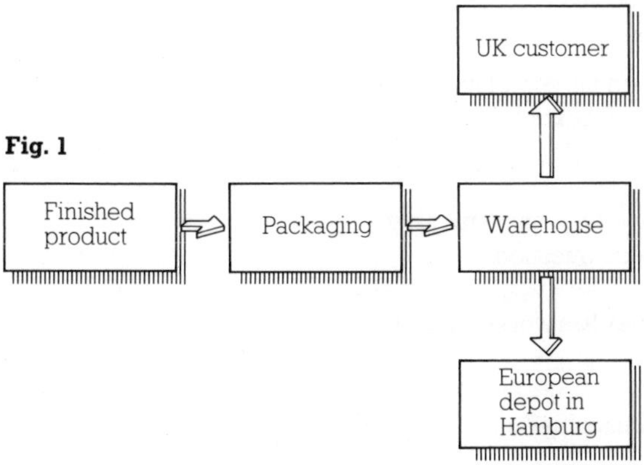

Fig. 2. HQ: Headquarters
F: Factory
D: Depot
C: Customer

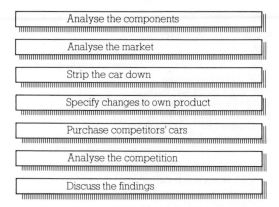

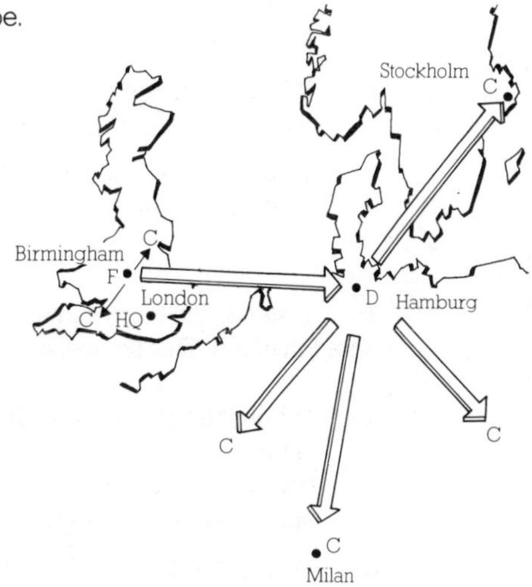

Fig. 1

One of TDC's customers in Stockholm has a serious complaint: 70% of the boxes containing the terminals in the last delivery have come open. 10% of the machines have been badly damaged.

a   What would the normal procedure be in a case like this?

b   Who should the customer contact? What action should be taken by TDC?

5 In the event this customer drafted a letter to be sent to the depot in Hamburg.

The objective of the letter was:

> to reflect their absolute dissatisfaction with TDC's service.
>
> to complain about the packaging in this order and in the last one, which was totally sub-standard.
>
> to inform TDC of their serious intention to look for a new supplier.

Read the draft. What changes would you make to emphasise the seriousness of their complaint?

Last week we received delivery of 200 boxes containing terminals. Unfortunately, some 70% of the boxes had burst open, and as a result 10% of the terminals were damaged. We suspect that the packaging may not have been up to the usual standard. This could be rather inconvenient for us as our stock of terminals is rather low, and we may not be able to meet all our outstanding orders.

We also feel we should point out that we were somewhat surprised at the high percentage of open boxes in our delivery last month. It would seem that your recent customer service is not quite of the standard we have come to expect from you. Therefore, we would appreciate your comments as soon as possible.

58   **6** *Listen to this conversation between John Stanley in the Packaging Department in the UK factory of TDC, and Tom Pitt, the Assembly Line Supervisor.*

a What action do you think will be taken concerning John Stanley's complaint?

b What is the connection between his complaint and the complaint from the customer in Stockholm?

7 Listen to the conversation between John Stanley and Tom Pitt again. This time answer these questions:

a When John Stanley says 'It never has worked properly', is he:
giving information?
showing that he is tired of the machine?

b When Tom Pitt says 'What's wrong this time?' is he:
really asking for information?
showing that he does not really want to hear?

c When Tom Pitt says 'Anyway, I thought that last time you managed to do it all by hand.' is he:
remembering what happened last time?
suggesting what Stanley should do this time?

The statements below were taken from a meeting called by the Managing Director of TDC (UK), Peter Jay, to discuss the loss of the Swedish customer and another major customer in Italy.

He is very critical of certain decisions which were taken, and mistakes which were made in the handling of complaints about packaging.

8 Complete the statements. Who do you think the criticisms are directed at?

a The packaging machine ... (REPAIR)

b You ... (REALISE) that packaging by hand isn't as efficient as machine packaging.

c It would have been better for us, if ... (INVEST) in a new machine instead of ignoring the problem.

d If the packaging machine ... (REPLACE) we ... (RECEIVE) so many complaints.

e We ... (HANDLE) the complaints more promptly.

f There ... (BE) a total lack of communication between the factory and Hamburg depot, or we would have found out what was going on sooner.

9 Act out extracts from this meeting in which Peter Jay questions the actions and decisions of the following:

the Manager of the Packaging Division
the Head of Customer Service
the Assembly Line Supervisor

FOCUS ON INTERACTION

Following TDC (UK)'s loss of two European customers in one week, the Americans have sent over one of their directors, Ray Bunsen, to find out what has happened. This is an extract from a meeting between Bunsen, Peter Jay, the UK Managing Director, and Bob Purvis, the UK Product Manager.

Meetings
59

1 Listen to the following dialogue and answer the questions.

a Jay says: 'Well, things could be a lot better.'
What does he really mean?

b Jay says: 'It looks as though ... It seems that ...'
Why does he use these expressions? What effect do they have?

c Bunsen says: 'I don't believe it.'
What does he mean by this?

d   Jay says: 'I know what you're saying, but this is a new operation here.'
What is his tactic? What is he trying to do?

e   Jay says: 'Damage must have happened in transit.'
Is he saying: It should have happened?
                It ought to have happened?
                It can only have happened?

f   Give three examples of aggressive statements.

g   Give two examples of defensive replies.

2   *Bunsen calls Carlo Corelli in Italy. This takes place before the meeting, when he is trying to gather information.*

Telephoning   Act out the telephone call, and when you have finished, listen
   to the dialogue on the tape.
60

3   Answer the following questions which relate to the dialogue.

a   What does Corelli say when he answers the phone?
Hullo, Mr Bunsen, I've ... call.

b   Bunsen wants to hear Corelli's explanation of the problem. What does he say?
I ... your ... things.

c   Bunsen doesn't let Corelli finish his explanation. What do you think he was going to say?
I can't get hold of ...

d   Bunsen asks Corelli if any action was taken by the factory concerning the complaint. What question does he ask?

e   How does Corelli emphasise that he doesn't think the damage occurred during shipping?

f   Bunsen uses two phrases in the latter part of the meeting which mean 'to get in contact again'. What are they?

4   Now act out a similar call from Bunsen to Inge Petersson in Stockholm.

ACTIVITIES

1   TDC (UK) is a company where information flow is totally inadequate. Bearing in mind what you already know about the company's activities, devise a system which will ensure that what happened with Corelli and Petersson never happens again.

John Stanley feels that the company should operate a system whereby information flows from the bottom to the top in a company, as well as information coming down the other way.

2a   Decide how you think such a system should work. How can this information be brought together?

b   What type of information should it be?

c   How should it be categorised and dealt with?

3   TDC (UK) is satisfied that it has now corrected the problems that caused the damage to the business. Write a letter to the depot in Hamburg explaining to them what they should do the next time they receive a complaint.

4   Phone Corelli or Petersson, and attempt to re-establish business.

5   Below is part of a report which was written by Ray Bunsen after his return from the UK to the USA. Complete the report, using the guidelines given. The words in **bold type** are instructions only. They show separate sections of the report.

I contacted both Inge Petersson in Stockholm and Carlo Corelli in Milan, to ask them for their side of the story. I was impressed by the similarity of their accounts. In both cases the deliveries contained boxes which had come open during transit, and as a result considerable damage had occurred. Most of this damage took place when the boxes were taken off the lorries, as several of them fell open and the terminals dropped out.

Summarise the problem
No information systems between customer/depot/factory/head office.

Detail what happened
Packaging machine broke down. Nothing was done.

Summarise the meeting with TDC (UK)

Summarise the new system to be implemented
Set out in detail the system you have devised in question 1.

6   Think of your own job situation, and of procedures where information flow is vital. Prepare a short presentation showing what this flow of information is and why it is important.

Case Study   3

Office automation

Salvo (Benelux) is the Belgian based subsidiary of a Swedish car manufacturer. The company language is English. The Swedish H Q has recently issued a directive that all subsidiaries should update and rationalise their office systems, particularly for word and data processing, and also look at areas where personnel can be reduced.

Salvo (Benelux) has therefore been instructed to analyse its general office automation needs, and to help them in this some specialists from the Swedish HQ have come to the company. Salvo (Benelux) already uses a large computer for payroll, accounts, invoicing, order processing and inventory control. The focus now is on ways in which word processors and micro-computers can be installed.

1   The Swedish specialists first step is to get different departments to think carefully about the job functions of people in that department. They therefore interview the managers of the following departments, among others, in order to ascertain how word processing and micro-computers can best be used:

> Marketing
> Personnel
> Office Administration
> Finance

Act out these interviews. The information is in the Teaching Guide.

The specialists decide to concentrate first on word processing applications. In order to decide which system is most suitable a sample of secretaries and typists is interviewed to find out what kind of work they do. At this stage the enquiry takes the form of a work study. The individual employees are not told the real reason for the interviews.

Based on the findings, the following chart is drawn up:

	0	1	2	3	4	5	6	7
	← Never					Always →		
Does the work involve frequent writing of reports?			✗					
Is the quality of document presentation very important?						✗		
Do you have to maintain constantly changing alphabetical lists?		✗						
Is the typical work repetitive with only minor variations?			✗					
Do peaks and troughs of work-flow create time management problems?			✗					
Does your typing requirement consist mainly of individual documents and telexes?						✗		
Does work need constant re-drafting?		✗						
Is your department involved in above-average typing loads, i.e. ten hours a day?			✗					
Do you retain and file large quantities of typed information for long periods?						✗		

The specialists then produce a report outlining the different types of word processing system that could be used, with advantages and disadvantages. They want to get the managers' reactions before recommending anything. Here is an extract from the report.

Re: Word Processing Systems for Salvo (Benelux)

The choice is basically between a stand-alone or a shared-resource system.

The stand-alone system, where each operator has a separate machine with its own micro processor and storage facilities, has the following advantages:

> It is cheaper to set up. Each machine costs about $9,000.
>
> It is flexible. Each office can have one and they can be moved around. No special room conditions are necessary.
>
> As the systems are not connected the breakdown of one does not affect the others.

There are also disadvantages:

> Access to data is relatively slow, and storage is limited.
>
> Each additional operator requires an additional system ($9,000).
>
> There will probably be a duplication of work and data stored on each system.

The alternative, a shared resource system, is more similar to a large computer system, with each operator having access through a terminal to a central computer where all data is stored. As many as 16 or 32 typists can use the system at once. Some of the benefits are:

> Vast quantities of text can be stored and accessed quickly by all operators.
>
> Cost of the system is spread over the number of terminals which are individually cheaper and less bulky than a full stand-alone system.
>
> Operators can be remotely supervised from one of the terminals.
>
> Each terminal can also do other computing work such as accounting, inventory control, etc.

Disadvantages also exist:

> An average price for a system with about 16 typists would be $90,000. However each extra terminal is relatively cheap.
>
> A machine breakdown could close down the whole system.
>
> A special room is needed for printing, and for the computer equipment.
>
> Operators must be within 1,000 meters of the central computer, otherwise communication must be by telephone lines and modems.
>
> As the equipment is complex, good technical and maintenance support is essential.

2   Based on the information given by the manager, and the chart drawn up after interviewing the secretaries and typists, what should the company choose and why?

How should they implement the new system?

One Year Later

The company has gone for a shared resource system as it seemed to offer more scope and potential than the stand-alone type. However there have been problems. Productivity has not increased as planned. Staff dissatisfaction is high, and a number of secretaries have left the company. Again some specialists from Sweden come down to try to find out what has gone wrong.

3   First they consult the managers who were interviewed a year before. Act out these interviews. The information is in the Teacher's Book.

61 🔊   **4**   They then interview some of the secretaries and operators. Listen to the extracts from two of these interviews.

5   On the basis of all the information decide where the company went wrong.

> Did it choose the wrong system?
> Was the system badly implemented?
> Were things properly planned?